Meeting Anthroposophy

Selected and Introduced by Robert Hill
Series Editor: Robert McDermott

CLASSICS FROM THE

Journal for
ANTHROPOSOPHY

NUMBER 79   MICHAELMAS 2008

This volume contains articles from the following issues of the
Journal for Anthroposophy:
Stephen Spitalny, 1999 (#69); Alan Howard, 1980 (#32);
Ann Steward, 1971 (#13); Michael Howard, 1997 (#64);
Annie Heuser, 1976 (#24); Van James, 1999 (#69);
Joel Morrow, 1985 (#40/41); Guus van der Bie, 1989 (#49);
Manfred Maier, 2000 (#71); Arvia Ege, 1975 (#21).

Cover painting: Ninetta Sombart
printed with the permission of Ninetta Sombart and Floris Books, publisher of
Ninetta Sombart: Life and Art by Volker Harlan, translated by Jon Madsen.
Originally published by Verlag Urachhaus (2004, Stuttgart, Germany)
Front cover and layout: Seiko Semones
Series editor: Robert McDermott
Editor and Introduction: Robert Hill
Copy editor and proofreading: Carol O'Brien
Journal for Anthroposophy
1923 Geddes Ave., Ann Arbor, MI 48104
TEL 734.662.9355 FAX 734.662.1727

ISSN-0021-8235

Printed by McNaughton & Gunn, Inc., Saline, Michigan

CONTENTS

Introduction
Meeting Anthroposophy*

Robert Hill

O ne of the most popular icebreakers when a group of anthroposophists gather is the question, "so how did you meet anthroposophy?" Depending upon how much time has passed since the initial encounter, the answer can take on more complexity and length. If you ask someone with an extensive acquaintance with anthroposophy, you might want to plan for a long answer, one that could have a number of chapters, with subplots and multiple layers. Think for a moment about your own response—your own story—and you will appreciate how much stands behind this seemingly innocent phrase. This "meeting" often connects with many threads in one's life and as one unravels them, a kind of personal mystery drama begins to emerge. You will probably realize in fact that it is a story that includes not one, but many "meetings."

With the phrase "meeting anthroposophy" we are using imagistic language, as if referring to an encounter with a person, not just with a body of work. We are giving, inadvertently at first, the term "anthroposophy" the status of a being. Certainly, for one's initial encounter(s), such an attribution is unintentional, just the casual use of a convenient figure of speech, but over time, as one's interest and connection grows, something unique begins to happen. A kind of ongoing dialogue or conversation is initiated. We are called upon to meet an anthroposophy that doesn't

---

* I would like to acknowledge with special thanks two individuals who read and offered valuable comments on this introduction: Hans Joachim Mattke and Nick Thomas. I also owe much to the editorial guidance and advice of Robert McDermott and to my frequent conversations with Louise Hill, whose insights have made this a much better essay.

remain static or knowable in the comfortable ways that other disciplines or bodies of knowledge are typically known.

We may find ourselves on some occasions and in some respects very drawn to anthroposophy, at other times confused, sometimes in agreement and sometimes in opposition. Each time a different meeting occurs, another face of anthroposophy is revealed that encourages us to challenge, doubt, affirm, and ultimately alter some of the basic views of ourselves and of the world that we think we know. It is this process of transformation and personal growth that draws us on. If we persist and adapt to the ever-changing interlocutor of anthroposophy, ever-new meetings await us, seemingly inexhaustible in number and content. We become engaged with an unfolding story that is at its base the mystery of ourselves, a story that has woven into it the karmic relationships that shape our lives and link us to our families, our friends, and ultimately to the world.

Of course, an infinite variation exists in the ways that individuals encounter anthroposophy, each appropriate to one's particular life situation, interests, relationships, and capacities. Yet, in spite of this seemingly infinite variation it is still possible to characterize these experiences in a way that can help us understand their mysterious power to reveal and transform. When I reflect on my own "meetings," I am struck by how different each one has been, and yet among them I find a strikingly similar quality, or continuity. They have taken on the character of subtle threshold experiences, doorways to new realities and to new ways of knowing.

In the present volume I have selected articles from the *Journal for Anthroposophy* that illustrate a variety of these meeting experiences. In this introduction I attempt to describe in a general way the challenges and opportunities for self-discovery they hold out to us and in so doing illustrate what I mean when I call them thresholds.

First Impressions

In reflecting on one's relationship with anthroposophy it is interesting to ponder: "At what point did I begin speaking of myself as an anthroposophist?" I remember feeling a certain sense of accomplishment and increased familiarity when I found it possible to pronounce the word *an-thro-pos-o-phy*. It took a bit of practice to get it right. How many times have you heard it mispronounced or garbled, usually by well-meaning friends or acquaintances? They act slightly offended by having to use it, as if it comes from a foreign language no one still speaks.

One of my favorite memories is of Francis Edmunds, founder and for many years director of Emerson College, beginning a lecture one evening to a large gathering of parents in a Waldorf school library. He stood in the middle of an open semicircular space, surrounded by parents. Some of them were suspicious of this word and what stood behind it. One could feel a tension building as Francis purposely stood almost a full minute before beginning his talk, waiting until there was absolute silence. Suddenly he spoke, with his inimitable English accent, in a clear ringing voice: "*An-thro-pos-o-phy,* wonderful word, *an-thro-pos-o-phy.*" It sent chills down the spine. He said the word with such reverence and yet with a kind of glee, as if he were inviting this special guest into the room. What followed was a talk that held every person in rapt attention for almost two hours. He paced and gestured as he spoke, meeting each person's eyes with a warmth and a directness that was transformative. Through Francis and through his delight and reverence for this "wonderful word" each person was given a marvelous opportunity to "meet anthroposophy," many for the first time.

Words matter when used in this way. To speak of oneself as an anthroposophist should carry a weight of responsibility that is palpable, which is why one tends to do so only after careful deliberation and only after one truly feels a kinship with the entity that stands behind this word. It isn't just a matter of the extent of one's exposure that determines whether one becomes comfortable with anthroposophy. I know people who have been associated with anthroposophical institutions for years who are still reluctant or unwilling to identify themselves as anthroposophists. They rightly see it as a momentous decision that should not be falsely made.[1] What threshold has one crossed when one speaks of oneself in this way? Stephen Spitalny in his essay "What is Anthroposophy?" uses a passage from Rudolf Steiner's *Anthroposophical Leading Thoughts* that begins to explain why this step feels so momentous:

> *He alone can acknowledge anthroposophy who finds in it what he himself in his own inner life feels impelled to seek. Hence only they can be anthroposophists who feel certain questions on the nature of*

the human being and the universe as an elemental need of life, just as one feels hunger and thirst. (p. 46)

There are certainly many who meet anthroposophy as one meets a long sought friend or life companion, with instant recognition and celebration. For such a person it is then a matter of renewing an acquaintance, refreshing a deep familiarity that only was waiting to be awakened. Yet even in such a case there is still a need for caution, for reflection, for moving forward with deliberation and full consciousness. One shouldn't assume too much, move too quickly and thereby create out of one's own comfort a barrier to deeper meetings.

For those, on the other hand, who find the word and the whole body of spiritual wisdom behind it to be daunting, or even threatening, is it ever possible to get past one's distrust and fear? For such individuals one of the only ways to meet anthroposophy is through an anthroposophist whom they have come to trust and respect, someone whom they can accept as a living validation of anthroposophy's rightful place in the world. In his celebration of the word and all that stands behind it, Francis Edmunds was doing much more than giving a philosophical lecture. He was inviting those in his audience, many of whom were skeptical, to meet anthroposophy in or through him. That night he did more than answer their philosophical questions; he gave them a living assurance of the right of anthroposophy to be in their school and in the world.

On more than one occasion I have heard anthroposophists described as "those people who have all the answers." This is of course not the impression one wants to leave with those whose interest is filled with skepticism, for it confirms rather than allays their anxious expectations. When someone brings to me a healthy (or even unhealthy) skepticism toward anthroposophy, it is crucial that she or he not find in me a person who espouses a system of beliefs, a dogma that answers or has a point of view on every question one might pose. If I respond as if I have all the answers, such a meeting becomes more about me than about anthroposophy. The person then experiences a version of anthroposophy that has become bound—"unfree"—by my personal ego. Unfortunately, he or she is likely to surmise that the opposite is the case, that anthroposophy holds me in its dogmatic prison. This would preclude, at least in that instance, a true meeting with anthroposophy.

The Language of Anthroposophy

Whether it be through reading one of the foundational books, working through a series of lectures, or attending an anthroposophical conference, one's initial exposure to anthroposophy is likely to entail coming to terms with an unusual and sometimes difficult vocabulary. As the pre-eminent example, Ann Steward begins her exploration of "The Geometry of Meditation" by calling our attention to the effect that the term "spiritual science" can have on our modern sensibilities. It works like a conceptual oxymoron, yoking together the two most sacrosanct and mutually exclusive worldviews of our time.

Spiritual science is a phrase that Rudolf Steiner and others use frequently and interchangeably with "anthroposophy." I believe it was his intention to challenge us to think in a different way about these two dimensions of human experience, to set us the task of comprehending them as a unified—not mutually exclusive—reality. With this term especially and with all of the foundational concepts of anthroposophy we are met unapologetically with a framework (threshold) that requires an act of imagination on the part of anyone who would pursue a serious study of the vast body of work it entails.

One of the central tasks of anthroposophy, Ann Steward maintains, is to resolve—or dissolve—the putative dichotomies set forth by the two competing worldviews referenced by the term "spiritual science," one espousing varying degrees of materialism and the other a spirituality that restricts itself to the domain of the inner life, usually according to a particular dogma or set of beliefs. She gives special attention to the work of the meditant who must overcome the bias that gives priority to—considers more real—the sense oriented spatial world over the inner or non-spatial realm of human consciousness. The student of spiritual science must not allow a bias toward either realm to influence one's scientific inquiry. One must apply, on the one hand, the scientific method with its rigor and objectivity of observation within the spiritual realm; on the other side, one must bring one's whole being with all of its capacities—physical senses, emotional intelligence, aesthetic sensibility, and spiritual awareness—to the study of the natural and mineral worlds.

To put in perspective the importance of the vocabulary of anthroposophy, consider for a moment an interesting reversal in perspectives. Suppose that the language of one of today's sciences, e.g., quantum physics, was not the accepted norm that purports to define the world as we know it. Suppose that we had not been exposed to the scientific language of quantum physics. How would we respond if suddenly confronted by such words as "quark," "photon," "neutron," or "wave-particle duality?" At the very least we would find such language confusing, perhaps exotic, even off-putting, ultimately raising one's skepticism and suspicion. You might well ask yourself if presented with a text or talk under those circumstances, using such language, "Why should I care about this, what bearing does it have on me or the world I live in? Why should I try to imagine these strange pictures or think these strange thoughts?"

The reality, of course, is that we know better, and because we recognize the validity and importance of this field of science, we do not ask these questions when exposed to its language. Even as scientific lay people we have come to accept that quantum physics has opened the door to some of the deepest secrets of the material world, conveying a body of knowledge that has radically altered the way we see and relate to the world. Its language has become the province of some of the greatest scientific minds, allowing them to explore the worlds of sub-nature in ways that would otherwise not be possible. To the prospective student of quantum physics, learning to speak and think its vocabulary represents a critical step in one's development before one can truly explore and contribute to its growing body of knowledge.

The vocabulary a scientist uses is essential for the precision, repeatability, and objectivity characteristic of scientific thinking. It enables a scientist to work within the tradition of knowledge that preceded his or her own work, and to convey the ideas and thought processes of one's research clearly and precisely. This language is critical for the creation of a reservoir of knowledge, accumulated over the life of a scientific field and available to those who would continue its work.

Such is also the case with spiritual science. Rudolf Steiner has bequeathed an extensive, precise vocabulary that he has drawn from the intellectual and cultural history of the West, from mystery traditions that have shaped the course of human development, and from the esoteric teachings of the world's great religions. Anyone who would become a serious student of anthroposophy will find his or her progress to be dependent on the use of its language. The facility with its vocabulary represents in itself the potential of deepening all subsequent meetings with anthroposophy. If one learns to "speak the language" of one's interlocutor, how much easier it is to know her.

Learning to Study Anthroposophy

During the first years of my study of Rudolf Steiner's writings and lectures, I sometimes found myself with conflicting feelings about what I had read. On the one hand I felt a deep appreciation for the remarkable wisdom contained in Steiner's works. On the other hand, I experienced a puzzling sense of frustration. After reading a lecture or a chapter from one of his books I naturally had a desire to hold on to what I had read, but after a short time—sometimes as little as a week—when I tried to recall the content, it seemed to have vanished. I could hardly recount a broad outline of it, much less its specific ideas or logical progression. The only solution was to read the text again, as if for the first time. It was frustrating because I was accustomed to retaining what I read. Having completed graduate degrees in the study of literature and having taught for a number of years I had trained myself to "make the text my own." Why couldn't I achieve the kind of control over a Steiner lecture that I found almost automatic with an essay in literary criticism? It was a puzzling dilemma.

For a long while I thought this problem must be due to a mistake that I was making, but then when I mentioned my conundrum to a few friends in a study group, several of them owned up to having a similar difficulty. I then began to query others and, to my surprise, found that many of them admitted to the same experience. I now realize that I stood before yet another threshold or "face" of anthroposophy that I had to decipher. It became apparent to me that many of us were making a fundamental error in the way we were reading Steiner's works and that I would have to learn to read or to study them in an entirely different way.

To be sure there are stylistic and structural explanations for the difficulty one has in reading a Steiner lecture. I could see this complexity, but over time I began to look for answers in an entirely different direction.[2] My line of inquiry, at first primarily intellectual, took on a more artistic direction under the influence of a number of mentors, including most importantly M. C. Richards who saw everything, including the act of reading a lecture, through the eyes of the artist.[3] This direction came as the revelation of a path of discovery that led to one of my most important "meeting" experiences. Studying anthroposophy became an adjunct to the meditative path that I learned about through that study, one reflecting and—over time—subtly changing the other. A type of inner dialogue was taking place, the substance of which I attempt to explain in this introductory essay.

While studying a particular lecture and working meditatively with its central ideas it occurred to me that, as with a work of art, one can miss its beauty and meaning by focusing solely on the detail, the parts, so to speak, of the work rather than on the whole. In reading a poem or a novel, mastering its language, its imagery, its thematic colors is but the doorway to the work itself. In order to truly know the work and the mystery of its artistry one has to meet it in a different way; one has to draw back and hold it in its totality within a meditative space for a period of time, as one might hold the presence of another person within oneself. What emerges from this process is akin to the revelation a Goethean scientist experiences through sensorial imagination, that is, a supersensory impression of the object or process one is studying; in this case an inner "meeting" can occur with that which gives the work of art its meaning, its identity, its power to affect one at the level of being. Through this meditative encounter the work comes alive in a way that transcends the intellect, which is altogether necessary in opening the door to the work, but can become an obstacle to meeting the artistic being of the work.

Michael Howard's precise description of the soul-spiritual process one experiences in the co-creation of beauty from a painting or sculpture also elucidates the process by which one meets the artistic being of a written work. In his essay "Art as Spiritual Activity" he gives us the following wonderfully succinct definition:

Beauty is an experience of the soul/spiritual as it shines through physical substance. However, our experience of beauty depends on an inner activity of living into the material medium in such a manner that the duality of physical and spiritual is transcended; in this way the physical is raised into the spiritual. (p. 66)

That which is akin to the beauty of a painting in a written or orally presented work is its "trueness"—not truth with a capital "T" but truth as an active working principle that shines through the wholeness of the work, even as beauty shines through a painting. This "trueness" comes to expression through the medium of one's own contemplative activity described above, transcending in this way the duality of part and whole. One's own individuality becomes the pigment or clay through which the work's truth manifests, thereby expressing that truth in infinitely varied, yet consistent ways that correlate with each person.[4]

As I thought more about this mystery of reading/studying anthroposophy, several of the ideas from Steiner's lectures began to coalesce. In the various descriptions Steiner gives of the nature of spiritual reality, he consistently points out that one's capacity to retain a supersensory experience in one's memory or as intellectual content, after the fact, is significantly diminished from what one is accustomed to with ordinary reality. Since one is *not* perceiving, or processing such an experience in the way one does in everyday reality—i.e., via the physical body, brain and neural pathways—it cannot be captured, or retained as we do ordinary memories and sense impressions. Because of this difference, such experiences will seem fleeting and elusive after the actual event itself has ended. They cannot be "re-membered," i.e., given the form of abstract thoughts or memories, in the same way that events that happen in the physical realm are held in memory.

I was beginning to appreciate Steiner's differentiation between the manifestation of an experience in the spiritual realm and that of an experience within the physical world. In the spiritual dimension, one is not separate from the experience in the way one is in the physical world. Within the spiritual realm one's knowing is through inclusiveness, through being within the experience of knowing. One's knowing becomes a perceiving rather than an act of contemplation and remembrance.

One's knowing comes not through a thinking-about, which requires and assumes a separation from and a distance between knower and object, but rather through placing one's awareness, the medium of one's thinking consciousness, within the perceiving-thinking process itself. In doing so, one's thinking consciousness becomes the organ of perception, rather than the organ for contemplating the perception. In the following passage from *An Outline of Occult Science*, Steiner describes the difference between the two kinds of reading experience:

> *While reading the communications concerning spiritual scientific knowledge, we live in a quite different manner than we do while reading those concerning external facts. If we read communications from the outer sense world, we are reading <u>about</u> them. But if we read communications about supersensible facts in the right way, we are living into the stream of spiritual existence.*[5]

The dilemma for a person who is learning to study an anthroposophical text has to do with the intellectual habits we have formed through many years of academic or independent study. One must learn to let go of the urge to retain and control intellectually what one reads. I realized that it was necessary to learn to read or study anthroposophy in a more active, participatory way. In *Saving the Appearances* Owen Barfield uses the term "participation" to refer to three phases of the evolution of consciousness. First he describes "original participation," a consciousness characterized by a complete unity between self and world.[6] Secondly, he describes the gradual loss of the capacity for direct experience, particularly as a result of the development of western rational and scientific objectivity. Barfield characterizes this middle phase as the time of the gradual loss of participatory consciousness. Finally, he uses the term "final participation" to convey the potential one has for experiencing this unity of self and world again, without abdicating or diminishing one's individuality. In our own time, he maintains, the potential exists for the whole of humankind to "participate" its union with the divine anew.[7] Such a state—"final participation"—corresponds to the perceptual or phenomenological thinking typical of the Goethean scientist when studying the natural world.

Through an act of sensorial imagination the scientist participates, or thinks-imagines (as opposed to thinking about) the object of one's study.

This act of thinking-perceiving requires that one relinquish or set aside the acute awareness of self that is a hallmark of modern consciousness, without letting go of one's individuality or presence as an individual consciousness. Through the deliberate, disciplined control of one's thinking consciousness, the focus on and awareness of self are set aside in order to make of one's thinking-consciousness a free space, wherein one can know-participate (directly know) instead of know about (indirectly) from the vantage point of one's separateness. Such an act of thinking engages the imagination in a precise way to create a living field of consciousness within oneself wherein the spiritual presence of what one is thinking-imagining becomes apprehensible, enabling a direct knowing rather than a knowing via the intellect once or twice removed from the object or idea known.[8]

Reading/studying anthroposophy, if one can approach it in this way, becomes an artistic act of co-creation, "a threshold experience," as Van James describes the artist's creative act in his essay "Art as a Threshold Experience."[9] Even in the earliest experiences of reading/studying anthroposophy one can sometimes get an inkling, a glimmer of "participatory" thinking. It comes in the form of the haunting feeling of familiarity one might have in reading a lecture or book for the first time, as if calling forth this knowledge out of oneself, awakening—participating—it in oneself rather than meeting it as separate from and perhaps alien to oneself. Such an experience gives one a taste, an echo of the quality of certainty that comes through the process of participatory or direct knowing. The effect upon oneself through this kind of knowing comes not at an abstract, twice or thrice removed level but at a level that touches one's very being, awakening one's will in ways that stir life forces within us. In Steiner's words: "Ideas become life-forces. We then have not just a knowledge of things, but we have made knowledge into a real organism, ruled by its own laws; the reality of our active consciousness has risen beyond a mere passive reception of truths."[10]

Through the study of anthroposophy it is possible to experience what Steiner characterizes as "living thinking." This shift or metanoia in one's way of thinking is a critical threshold that leads to a "meeting" with anthroposophy as being rather than as abstract ideas. In his essay "*Like Shadows We Are . . .*" Alan Howard gives a clear depiction of the process of the transformation of thinking that is possible through the study of anthroposophy. He sees the development of the capacity for "living" or "participative" thinking as nothing less than the way out of "Plato's cave," wherein one's consciousness is confined to the shadows of abstract (intellectual) thinking. In the following passage he establishes the relationship between this direct way of knowing and the three capacities that constitute our higher human nature, all of which become fully engaged through "living thinking": the capacity to think, the capacity to love, and the capacity to act morally:

> . . . *it is a matter of transforming the knowing process. It is a change from knowing as an intellectual process, to knowing as a moral deed.*
>
> *And that deed is Love; not love in any of the sentimental or self-seeking ways in which it is so often represented, but love as the selfless reception of another being. Love is giving up oneself to receive another being into oneself. It is the organ of cognition of being. The intellect can only take us up to the point where love becomes possible. Beyond that it has to sacrifice itself as intellect; and, emptying itself of self, let the other live, become known, in that emptied self.* (p. 53)

The outcome for the individual who can bring these three aspects of oneself into the unified activity of knowing is human freedom, which leads—in the context of Alan Howard's essay—to a release from "Plato's cave."

How Did Rudolf Steiner Meet Anthroposophy?

After reading Annie Heuser's essay "Goetheanism Resurrected in Anthroposophy," it is interesting to ask a kind of inverse question to her implied theme: "Did Goethe's scientific writings play a role in awakening the impulse for spiritual science in Rudolf Steiner?" or more generally, "How did Rudolf Steiner meet anthroposophy?" This question is intriguing not just for its biographical significance, but because in answering it we may gain important insights regarding our own threshold/meeting experiences with anthroposophy.

Annie Heuser emphasizes how important it was for Rudolf Steiner to integrate his own spiritual scientific work with the cultural and scientific life of the late 19th century. In her essay she explains why, or more importantly how, Goethe exemplified that link for Steiner. In addition to the indisputable part Goethe played in the cultural life of Europe, Goethe's scientific thinking became the point of departure from which Steiner would launch his own epistemological and scientific exploration: "Goethe succeeded in working his way through from mere erudition 'to a human world-conception', the cognitive foundation of which Rudolf Steiner was able to illumine." It will be useful in this study to trace the moment or moments of insight—the epiphanies—in Steiner's young adult life that led to his groundbreaking work toward illuminating Goethe's process of cognition. These moments could well represent early thresholds of insight that opened the way for Steiner to the path of knowing he called anthroposophy.[11]

According to the autobiographical account of his early twenties, Steiner supplemented the rigorous curriculum of his technical college education by attending many additional courses in the natural and physical sciences and through extensive independent reading and study.[12] We know from his subsequent lecture series that his knowledge of the scientific and philosophic thought of his time was deep and broad. He was clearly deter-mined to be erudite in these disciplines, but in becoming so he would create in himself a steadily building sense of unease, an internal dilemma that would cry out for resolution. In many instances his spiritual insights were at odds with the knowledge he acquired in these disciplines. In spite of this uneasiness, he tells us that in all of his academic and extracurricular work he was meticulous in meeting the subject matter as it was presented without calling it into question on the basis of his spiritual acuity.

> . . . I never allowed my spiritual insight to interfere with acquiring knowledge of the sciences as they were then presented. I applied myself to what was taught, and only at the back of my mind was there always the hope that one day the union of natural science and knowledge of the spirit would reveal itself to me. (p. 32)

The key ideas that would solve his dilemma came not from the sciences but from his reading of Schiller's *Letters on the Aesthetic Education of Man*.[13] No doubt because of the growing dichotomy Steiner was experiencing within himself, he was "greatly stimulated" by Schiller's characterization of the two pivotal states of human consciousness (p. 34). Schiller distinguishes between the state of consciousness that is oriented toward the sensory, natural world and that which is concerned with the inner world of reason and moral conscience. Moreover, it is through the "aesthetic education" of the individual, Schiller asserts, that it becomes possible to permeate the first type of consciousness with that of the second, enriching one's interaction with the sensory world through engaging the higher capacities of the human being—reason and moral conscience. This interpenetration of the "lower" with the "higher" consciousness engenders an intermediate state—"an aesthetic disposition"—which, Schiller maintains, is the consciousness by means of which the human being becomes the artist, creating and experiencing beauty in all its forms.

Encountering Schiller's theory of human consciousness at this time in his development led to one of Steiner's most important epiphanies. On the basis of his own spiritual insights, he realized that Schiller was describing the "crossing point" between perceptual/conceptual thinking and the spirit, thereby pointing the way to a resolution of the enigma of consciousness that troubled his own inner life.[14] This realization would open the door for Steiner to a revelatory new mode of scientific inquiry. "Is it not possible," he asked himself, "to consider such a state of consciousness for mediating the truth in the nature of things?" (p. 34) Human consciousness, he realized after reading Schiller, must "attain a certain condition before its relationship with the world accords with the true nature of the human being."

> *This aesthetic disposition allows the soul to live through the senses but brings something spiritual to physical perception and to our actions stimulated by the sensory world. We then perceive with our senses as though they were permeated with spirit. (p. 34)*

Steiner was being presented with a way to dissolve the dichotomy between the external world as presented by science and the interpenetrating world of spirit, which he experienced directly and intimately. It was also discernable to him that "such a state of consciousness is realized to a certain degree when we not only entertain thoughts that portray external things and events, but when we have thoughts that we experience as the thoughts themselves" (p.35). From this initial revelation he would bring to full clarity an understanding of the relationship of human thinking to spiritual perception, including the remarkable insight that would serve as the basis of his foundational work *The Philosophy of Spiritual Activity*.[15] He discerned that thinking when turned upon itself, serving simultaneously as organ of perception and object of perception, becomes the perceptual doorway to the spiritual activity of human consciousness. This marks a threshold experience in every sense of the word for Rudolf Steiner.

> *A spiritual perception was disclosed to me not through vague mystical feeling, but through spiritual activity that is fully comparable in clarity to mathematical thinking. I approached a state of consciousness that allowed me to justify my perception of the world of spirit, even to the forum of scientific thinking. I was in my twenty-second year when I had these experiences. (p. 35)*

This experience would prepare Rudolf Steiner for his groundbreaking work on Goethe's scientific research and serve as a harbinger for the significant contributions to epistemology he would make in subsequent years.

This experience answers the question as to how Rudolf Steiner met the spiritual stream of wisdom he would name anthroposophy. It gives us a vivid picture of the "meeting" experience that would launch his life's work, bridging the realms of spirit and science. It also reveals what may be the critical element, the *sine qua non*, of any true meeting with a spiritual stream of wisdom such as anthroposophy. Reaching a certain "state of consciousness" precipitated this threshold experience for Rudolf Steiner. What was the nature of this state of consciousness, what was its cause or origin, and what role might such a state play in our own meeting experiences? These are questions we can attempt to answer on the basis of Rudolf Steiner's experience.

Firstly, what created the state of consciousness in Rudolf Steiner that enabled his epiphany? The spiritual world was for him a tangible, ever present reality; the capacity to perceive/experience the spirit within the objective world was a given. What he had to develop in himself was the capacity to see reality as everyone else saw it. He had to develop a thorough knowledge of the world as seen and thought by the best minds of his time. In doing so he would create a deeply felt tension in himself between the two apparently disparate realities of spirit and matter, of scientific and spiritual knowledge. His biography had fostered in him an acute awareness of the crossing point of the physical and the spiritual worlds. Thus, he prepared in himself a "state of consciousness" that held in delicate balance his newly gained knowledge of orthodox science and his spiritual perceptions, not allowing either perspective to be the basis of a judgmental negation of the other. He had maintained in himself a space that was free of preconceived, ego-based perceptions about the relationship between these two worlds. Such a "state of consciousness" prepared him for the encounter with Schiller's depiction of the "aesthetic consciousness," which then served as the impetus for the "meeting/threshold" perception Steiner depicts in his autobiography.

At this point in his life Rudolf Steiner was preparing to begin his work with Goethe's scientific writings. It was almost certainly not coincidental that the enabling condition of his own breakthrough discovery—"*a state of consciousness that allowed me to justify my perception of the world of spirit, even to the forum of scientific thinking*"—would also lead him to his core insight into Goethe's scientific methodology, the determinate role of the scientist's own state of consciousness, both as preamble to a study of nature's mysteries and as organ of perception through which those mysteries reveal themselves. Annie Heuser also makes this connection, but in a slightly different way. She shows that Rudolf Steiner has resurrected Goetheanism by assimilating its underlying epistemology and its scientific methodology into anthroposophy's two primary streams of knowing—living thinking and spiritual scientific inquiry.

In the context of establishing this linkage between Goetheanism and anthroposophy, Heuser makes an astute observation in her comparison of Goethe's path of development with that of Rudolf Steiner. Her comment sheds additional light on the nature of the state of consciousness that can lead to a meeting/threshold experience. She compares the trajectory of their respective life paths, with emphasis on the origin of those paths:

> *Starting out from a true knowledge of nature, Goethe climbs to a grasp of the being of man. Rudolf Steiner's life-path leads from the spirit-world, which at no time was closed to him, to an experience*

of the world of ideas. (p. 76)

The path of development for most of us will follow a trajectory that is closer to Goethe's than to Steiner's. Our orientation is the world of materialism, the world of orthodox science, which has pounded into our heads the conviction that what we experience through our senses is the only verifiable reality. Intellectually, we can certainly entertain the possibility of other dimensions, but the reality we know and trust is the material world. When we encounter anthroposophy we begin with a point of view that sees the spiritual realm as beyond the reach of our perceptual modality and therefore is unknowable in any direct way. All of this is to say that for an individual living today the starting point on the path of development is diametrically opposite to that of Rudolf Steiner. One's path today might be described as the inverse of Steiner's path of development.

Steiner's knowledge of the spiritual world equaled in its certainty our knowledge of the material world. His task was to attain the same confidence and facility with knowledge of the physical, material world, whereas our task is to attain knowledge of the spiritual world while retaining our orientation and capacities within the material realm. To do this we must develop the capability to open within ourselves a receptive "state of consciousness" that is free of bias and open to a new way of perceiving, thinking, and feeling. We must follow Steiner's example, but in reverse. With good reason, Steiner begins many of his lectures with an appeal that his audience receive what he is presenting with unbiased, open minds. His statement often is given no more than a casual affirmation—"sure I can maintain an open mind. I do it all the time at my job or listening to my spouse." Yet the import of his request is far greater than this trivial example; he means that we actually should listen to or read his words with a different "state of consciousness," one that we must learn through much practice and a willingness to entertain a radically different vision of reality. It is a precondition if we are to meet anthroposophy as a stream of living knowledge that touches our full humanity. Van James invokes the image of the blank canvas as a picture of the threshold that the artist confronts in the act of bringing spirit into view. It is an apt image for the state of consciousness that we must create in ourselves as we seek new meetings with anthroposophy.

We must learn to think the thoughts of spiritual science—even as Rudolf Steiner learned to think the thoughts of material science—through the medium of a radically different mode of consciousness, one that is receptive to ideas as active, living forces that touch us at the level of our will and our whole being. Then we too can achieve the synthesis of spirit and matter, thinking/perceiving not two worlds but one unified realm of matter permeated by spirit.

Meeting Anthroposophy in the World

A growing number of opportunities exist in much of the world today where one can encounter anthroposophy in ways that are, on the one hand, direct or intentional, and, in contrast, that are inadvertent or by chance. The possibility for both kinds of encounter is a consequence of the dual stance of anthroposophy in the world. Its most direct and visible "footprint" is the Anthroposophical Society, which I will take up in the concluding section of this introduction. A less direct presence is through works arising from the spiritual science of anthroposophy that affect the practical aspects of everyday life. Parents who are looking for the best possible education for their children enroll them in a Waldorf school; a family who wants fresh produce grown according to the healthiest methods joins a local community garden where the farmers are following an holistic approach to agriculture called Biodynamics; individuals interested in new art forms attend the performance of a novel form of movement called eurythmy, while someone else with a persistent medical problem is directed to a clinic where this same form of movement has been modified to serve as a unique form of therapy. The purpose of these anthroposophical initiatives is to provide critical services and benefits to those who have need of them, without overt reference to their source of inspiration.

The list of possibilities covers a diverse range of practical and consequential work in education, the sciences, the arts, in the fields of medicine and therapy, within societal and financial institutions, in the renewal of religious ritual, in the care and education of handicapped children and adults; the list could continue at some length. One need not be a proponent of—or even be aware of—anthroposophy to benefit from this continually expanding network of services, accessible to a wide range of constituencies. Unlike belief systems that have a visible and shaping influence on the services offered under their auspices, there is no inherent intentionality within anthroposophy to use these initiatives as platforms for promoting its teachings. The absence of a proselytizing motive may appear ironic, since it is largely through these practical avenues that the largest number of lives are touched or affected, in some cases profoundly.

Anthroposophy is not a religion, a sect or a movement in search of converts, but in its purest form a path of knowing, a spiritual science. When encountering the term "spiritual science" a common tendency is to discount the import of the word "science" and to conflate "spiritual" with a religious belief system. This inclination is understandable within a public arena where the majority of educational, professional, and cultural institutions subscribe to a bifurcation of reality, as discussed earlier. Initiatives arising from the spiritual teachings and spiritual science of anthroposophy counter this image of reality not by promoting and proselytizing for a contrary belief system, but through their stance in the world as the consequential outcomes of a path of knowing that heals the schism in the human being and in the human community. Those who benefit from such endeavors meet as a working principle, albeit indirectly, a path of knowing that integrates—desegregates—the spiritual and the physical within the human being and the world.

The relationship one has to the works arising from the spiritual scientific method could be compared to the way one relates to the benefits derived from traditional science. One need not be a scientist, or even have a layman's knowledge of the sciences, to benefit from their discoveries. Likewise, with the outcomes of the work done on the basis of the spiritual scientific method, one can accept the fruits of this research at face value and leave it at that, or one can make the intentional effort to inquire about what stands behind these initiatives. If one chooses to take such a step, it can begin a process of personal exploration and study. For most, such exploration will simply satisfy their curiosity; for some it may inspire a deep continuing inquiry, possibly leading eventually to a change of vocation.

If one does undertake a path of study, it can begin a series of meetings with anthroposophy of the kind described above that will reconfigure how one sees and knows the world. It may be more accurate in this case to speak not of meeting anthroposophy in the world but of *meeting the world through anthroposophy*. What before was unknowable and devoid of spirit becomes a realm infused with a complex array of spiritual being and beings. A transposition of one's point of view gradually occurs, reshaping the relationship one has with the world and with oneself. Through these meetings—threshold experiences—one is challenged to change not only one's thoughts about the world but one's *way* of thinking about the world. Instead of seeing it through the lens of preconceived conceptual snapshots as an external observer, one is called upon to develop the capacity to participate—directly know—the world as process coming into being.

In the collection of essays that follow, several of the works demonstrate the transposition of thinking that distinguishes spiritual science from traditional scientific inquiry. Two in particular illustrate this difference: Joel Morrow's quest to find a form of agriculture that fosters a participative harmony with the rhythmic processes of nature, and Dr. Guus van der Bie's study of the polarity of the heart rhythm. In each case we see an individual who has become a practitioner of spiritual science within a well-established vocational/scientific discipline—agriculture and medical science. Their respective essays illustrate the transposition of perspectives that has occurred for each as a result of his study/practice of spiritual science. A shift has taken place in the site of their thinking consciousness and soul-spiritual activity, moving from an analytical or "extensive" point of view—*outside* the phenomenon—to an "intensive" presence *within* the phenomenon.[16]

For Joel Morrow such a transposition of perspectives is critical to the realization of "a new vision of nature." He knows that he must find a means of working with the earth that will allow the scientist or farmer to live/know the rhythmic processes of nature with the intimacy of the old-world peasant farmer. A pivotal experience in Joel's life with this way of living/knowing came in the person of his friend and mentor Margarete Lueder. She consciously had cultivated an "intensive" (peasant-like) relationship with the rhythmic processes of nature through her lived knowledge of biodynamic agriculture. As he observed and admired her intimate relationship to the cycles of the year and to the rhythms of dying and coming-into-being of the natural world, he understood that she embodied a way of knowing the world and its processes from the "inside." One's thinking must become, he saw, "like the living world it contemplates. … thoughts must become plants." (p. 90) He finds this "intensive" way of knowing also in Goethean science, as practiced by scientists like Jochen Bockemühl. Before "a new vision of nature" can be a reality for the biodynamic farmer or the Goethean scientist, he concludes, thoughts must become forces of will that arise according to the cycle of the year, weaving into one's being the wisdom of nature and into one's knowing her secrets.

Dr. Guus van der Bie, MD, presents a picture of the heart that is simultaneously supersensible and physical. Rather than segregating the spiritual mythology of the heart from the science of cardiology—relegating the spiritual to a purely metaphorical status—Dr. van der Bie marries the two perspectives. The resulting spiritual scientific study of the polarity of the beating heart sheds the light of science on the heart's spiritual function and applies the knowledge of the spirit to the science of cardiology. Out of his study comes a new vision of the heart as spiritual activity. The polarity of the heart rhythm reveals itself to be the formative polarity that informs human existence: at the systole (contracting) or higher pole, consciousness arises through the sacrifice of life substance, while at the diastole (expanding) or lower pole, life-renewal comes through sacrificing the light of consciousness. The most critical point in this rhythmic process is the moment of "pole reversal." At this instant the heart serves as "an organ of the turning points of time," (p. 101) a portal to supersensible worlds. One might also see it as a moment of transposition when the physical heart ("outside") becomes the spiritual heart ("inside"). At the mid-point of its polarity the heart becomes the organ of supersensible perception that enables the human being to receive/participate higher knowing. It becomes the place of meeting with anthroposophy.

Meeting the world through anthroposophy is transformative of ourselves and the world. In developing the capacity to participate the world through our study and practice of anthroposophy we become responsive and responsible for creating the world in our image as human beings, and in taking into ourselves the being of the world.

Impediments to Meeting Anthroposophy

Through one's meetings and work with anthroposophy one becomes increasingly conscious of the spiritual or supra-natural aspects of oneself and the world. Even though the realm of the supra-natural is non-spatial and not directly perceivable to the physical senses, it is directly knowable through the heightened capacity of "living thinking," as discussed in this introduction. We also are exposed to many encounters with the realm of sub-nature, including the electrical systems and appliances that surround us constantly, the advanced technologies used to diagnose and treat our medical problems, and all of the electronic media that entertain us, keep us connected, and drive the realms of business and commerce. Ironically, this is a part of the physical, material world that mimics the spiritual or supra-natural world in one important respect. Under normal circumstances—without the assistance of sophisticated technological aids—the phenomena of sub-nature are outside of our sensory purview. They are invisible, inaudible, non-tactile, and without smell or taste; in other words, they exist outside the range of our conscious awareness. However, the phenomena of sub-nature in contrast to supra-natural phenomena are readily acknowledged by traditional scientific criteria as an ever present, quantifiable, and eminently knowable part of everyday life.

While the existence of sub-nature is readily accepted by almost everyone, rarely do we take note of the presence of sub-natural phenomena in our lives. We are certainly aware of their effects as manifested through the technologies that support and shape our working, living, and social environments. Their impact is substantial in definitive ways that can be simultaneously positive and detrimental over the whole spectrum of human life. It is not my intention to examine the full range of these effects—such as the permeation of the space around and within us by continuous streams of radio and electromagnetic waves of varying frequencies. This could merit an article if not a book length project in itself. What is of interest in the context of this introduction is the remarkable degree to which visual, audio, communications, and computer technologies—powered and conducted by sub-natural phenomena—have become the media and the medium of an imaginary world that has largely displaced or replaced the spiritual dimension of our lives.

When engaged through the Internet the combined effect of electronic media is to create the compelling fantasy of a world within a world that gives the illusion of being outside the dimensions of time, space, and materiality. It is an imagined realm with the apparent qualities of simultaneity, omnipresence, and virtuality. One's communications and contact with anyone or any point in the world appear essentially simultaneous; one's cyber (computer) presence can give the impression of being anywhere and everywhere; while one's actual presence within this media-created "cyberspace" is nowhere, i.e., virtual. These are qualities that seem to defy the constraints of reality, offering superhuman connectivity to information, access to the media and entertainment in all its forms, apparently unlimited ability to participate in cyber relationships and cyber communities, the power to make one's opinion or voice heard to almost anyone connected to the web, and instantaneous access to a broad assortment of information and knowledge in a variety of forms.

With its cyber-power, the Internet seems to bestow super-human capabilities upon its users within this imaginary realm. Even the supreme act of re-creating oneself is made "virtually" possible. One can give cyber-birth to an alter ego imagination, either through a software program like "MySpace" or, in a more extreme form, by creating a virtual "object" called an "avatar," which becomes an animated version of the user. With the help of an elaborate software program called "Second Life," one's avatar takes on a virtual existence within a cyber "metaverse" that is jointly "participated" by other player "residents" through their avatars.[17] The popularity of such programs reflects the growing power of the media—in particular the Internet—to control and shape even the personal, intimate aspects of the lives of its users. Their power and appeal expose deeply seated unmet needs of their users, which software designers clearly understand and exploit.

For many people such programs have become an obsession, absorbing the vitality and reality from their everyday life. While one's interest in and focus on the reality of one's existence diminishes, one's avatar grows in its cyber vitality, until it threatens to become one's raison d'etre. As this occurs, the roles of creator and created may become reversed, allowing an illusory cyber world that one "participates" to become the primary locus of one's existence. In this instance, one has crossed a different kind of threshold, not into the realm of spiritual knowing, but into the realm of the sub-human, meeting/participating an alter ego created out of lower desires and ambitions.

The term cyberspace is a misnomer; it is not a space at all but a carefully crafted fantasy of a supra-natural domain that entwines the world in a cyber—computer—generated "worldwide web." The science fiction writer William Gibson has described cyberspace famously as "a consensual hallucination experienced daily by billions . . ."[18] If one makes the conscious effort to extract oneself from the illusionary power of the fantasized web,[19] it is readily apparent that this world within a world is not at all what it appears to be. It is instead a legerdemain performed by sophisticated computer software that manipulates a complex maze of electronic switches according to the logic of binominal mathematics. Through sophisticated mathematical algorithms written in one of many complex symbolic codes, software programs drive an invisible technology that hides its mechanisms behind enticing visual and auditory illusions that lull a person into comfortable acceptance of a cyber/computer "space" that does not exist. The de facto interior space of the Internet is filled with computer components, silicon microchips, transmitters, electrical circuitry, millions of miles of optical cables and electrical wiring, and assorted other mechanical and electrical gadgetry, all serving the purpose of conducting and transmitting electrical signals and electromagnetic waves over a broad range of frequencies.

The remarkable acceptance of the fantasy of cyberspace by literally billions of people gives it the linguistic and perceptual status of a "collective representation," in this case a "collective mis-representation."[20] It is real because it is perceived to be real by virtually everyone. The mechanism by which this new feature has been added to our worldview is the substitution of an "extensive" (physical) reality for an "intensive" (spiritual) reality. This astonishing misapprehension is possible largely because so many of the billions who conceive or cognize what is not there are not able or willing to distinguish between the "extensive" and the "intensive" dimensions within themselves or within the natural world. A prime example is the tendency to misapprehend the interior of one's own body—brain waves, neurons, heart, internal organs, muscles, etc.—as the "intensive" dimension of one's self and one's consciousness—"I am my brain"—while in reality it is but another aspect of the "extensive" dimension of the body.

The mechanized, electronic interior of the Internet is the hidden or forgotten space wherein the forces of sub-nature work their magic, out of sight and out of reach of the sensory grasp and conscious awareness of the billions of people who continuously take advantage of their power, effectively blinded by the "collective representations" of cyberspace and the worldwide web. Our ignorance of this interior, extensive reality— hidden in plain sight—seems an apt example of the state of unconsciousness depicted in the passage from the *Gospel according to Matthew* cited by Manfred Maier at the beginning of his essay: "You hear with your ears but do not understand; you see with your eyes but do not perceive. The hearts of human beings have become lifeless and dull. Their ears are hard of hearing and eyes are tired." An inability to distinguish between the "intensive" and "extensive" dimensions of one's human nature closes all possibility for meeting/threshold experiences since one has been programmed not to "see" or acknowledge the existence of an intensive/spiritual aspect of the human being.

Granted, the "work" done by sub-nature is substantial, affecting all facets of human life. So great in fact are the advantages and advances we glean from their presence in our lives that we overlook or forget to notice their detrimental effects, in particular on our most human attributes. The comfortable illusions of cyberspace, without one's notice, can have a powerful anesthetizing effect on one or all of the critical constituents of one's human identity—on one's thinking life, feeling life, or on one's volition. If the integrity or vitality of any of these attributes is compromised, the foundation of one's human identity is put at risk. It then becomes much easier for one's ego to be co-opted, making one more a servant or adjunct to this cyber-world than one who is being served by it.

With one's thinking, it is critical to exercise as much clarity, control and self-awareness as possible when engaging any of the media technologies— film, television, audio, communication technologies, and especially the Internet. One should be alert to any indications that one's thinking consciousness is being dulled or co-opted, such as the weakening or loss of the faculty for critical judgment—one's ability to distinguish between objectivity and distortions. Over time a persistent haziness or resistance to being fully awake or alert can begin to take over one's consciousness. It becomes comfortable and easy to relax into the stream of media sensations, allowing them to flow without resistance or questions through one's consciousness. This feeling can escalate to a type of intoxication that holds one captive, with no will or desire to turn off or away from the TV, Internet, iPod, iPhone, or Blackberry device. One's own spiritual activity is put into sleep mode, giving over one's nervous system and sensory pathways literally to the transmissions emanating from the media. One becomes plugged-in, converted into an adjunct of the electronic stream of media consciousness. What was an "intensive" dimension of one's self has become an "extensive" dimension of the electronically-driven media. The inner (intensive) life of those who are victimized in this way has been displaced/replaced by an extensive electronically borne media consciousness.

Recent research on the brain's plasticity has established that one's thinking consciousness can have a physiological effect on the brain itself, shaping or reshaping not only one's thoughts but also the neurological pathways of the brain that enable those thoughts.[21] Allowing one's thinking consciousness to be incapacitated or co-opted by our media saturated environments can all but eliminate the potential for conscious spiritual activity—"living thinking"—as characterized by Rudolf Steiner and briefly described in this introduction. In contrast, developing the capacity and state of consciousness that enables "living thinking" will have a formative effect in the opposite direction, strengthening and clarifying one's thinking consciousness as an organ of higher perception. One's human capacities can be strengthened and can preserve one's sense of individual integrity or wholeness. "Living thinking" becomes in this way an intensive (spiritual) and extensive (physiological) antidote to the effects of the media illusions created by means of sub-natural phenomena.

One's feeling life is equally at risk from the invasiveness of media saturation. One's feelings provide the basis of what is commonly referred to as emotional intelligence, a different type of sensory/cognitive system that is of vital importance to one's awareness of self and to one's sensibility toward others. One's artistic sensibilities, moral compass, capacity for selfless actions, all arise from one's feeling life. This under-appreciated element of one's humanity is the basis for an individual's capacity to build relationships and to be a functioning member of a human community. A healthy, balanced feeling life gives one the potential to transcend and transform one's egocentric perspective, literally by sensing and cognizing the presence of another within the intensive space of oneself.

The impact of living in a world supersaturated with a constant stream of emotionally laden music, language, imaginations, commercial exaggerations, and media entertainment can be devastating to one's cognitive feeling life. A few symptoms to take note of as indicators that one's emotional intelligence is at risk include: a growing tendency to live one's life vicariously through the artifice of film, TV, or the Internet, to the point of sometimes losing track of who or what is fictional and what is real; becoming a consumer whose dress, diet, health, work habits, relationships, entertainment, and financial decisions are largely shaped by the norms or standards promoted via the consumerism of the commercial media; altering one's values and belief system on the basis of the evangelical media or politically biased newscasts; dependence upon the media "mind" to the point of feeling disoriented and not one's self if deprived of its stimulation for a period of time. One can become addicted to a constant stream of media stimulation, overloading one's feeling sensory system with a false or illusory sense of what it means to be human, distorting and ultimately replacing one's sense of self with an artifice created and maintained by the technologies of sub-nature.

Finally, the ultimate "temple" of human individuality is volition, one's capacity to act in the world, to decide for oneself what to think and what should and should not be a fixture in one's life and in one's consciousness. An ever-present threat to that temple for most of us is the growing addiction that our society as a whole has to electronic media, in all its forms and variations. Even children—or one should say *most of all* children—are at risk. Beginning at the toddler stage, children spend their lives in a constant stream of media stimulation. Some form of media serves as babysitter, as placating (mesmerizing) entertainment, as substitute teacher, or even as substitute parent, and finally as a cyber window through which children see a two dimensional artificial world from which they form their perceptions and conceptions of reality.

As adults we are almost certainly addicted to some degree to one or more of the media. We have become a compulsive generation of media dependents who feel anxious, incomplete, deprived, inadequate, or somehow at risk without continuous connectivity via a multitude of media tools and systems. If you doubt whether this could possibly include yourself, consider the following questions, which may expose your media addictive tendencies. Do you find yourself automatically turning on the TV, radio, or Internet first thing in the morning not long after waking? Is it difficult to turn off the TV or the Internet, especially at night before turning in? Do you often find it hard to stop the media-generated conversations that go on ad infinitum in your mind, keeping you from going to sleep, or do you wake up in the middle of the night and find it hard to go back to sleep, so you end up watching TV, turning on your computer and tapping into the Internet or checking your email? Are you always checking your email, or wondering whether you have unread email? How many mobile electronic systems do you own or carry with you—mobile phones, Blackberry like devices, iPods, microcomputers, etc.? Do you find yourself at a loss, not knowing what to do next without some form of media playing in the background, plugged into your ears, or occupying your mind? As with any form of obsessive dependency, media addiction can take over one's life, paralyzing one's ability to alter the patterns of one's behaviors, and ultimately one's consciousness. For those who suffer from it—and most of us do to some degree—it becomes a compulsion that one has to fight against practically for the rest of one's life. An interesting question to ponder is whose will is controlling us when we turn automatically to the media, for whatever reason?

The remarkable extent to which the Internet (a.k.a., the worldwide web) has become available to anyone with a computer and minimal user skills makes this illusory experience of "cyberspace" a commonly shared daily event for a large portion of the world's population. It has become in this regard a kind of faux "crossing of the threshold of all of humankind." Rudolf Steiner refers to such an actual threshold experience as an imminent event in humankind's evolutionary development. He is referring to an increasing accessibility to spiritual phenomena for all of humankind in the 20th and 21st centuries. Examples of this occurrence would be the "meeting/threshold" experiences discussed in this introduction. However, as Manfred Maier points out, this increased opportunity to experience/participate the spiritual—intensive—dimension of reality will be unrealized, remaining a subconscious or suppressed longing that is not fulfilled if this access is cut off or replaced by a substitute, illusory replica. As a result, the threshold experience that a large portion of humankind unknowingly may turn toward is the lower world of sub-nature rather than that of the higher realm of the spirit. The consequences of this substitution would be an awakening of the lower instinctual side of the human being in place of the development of higher spiritual capacities. The electronic media in all its forms, and most especially the "worldwide web," can be the instruments of just such a contravention of the intended course of evolutionary development—for the individual and for humankind.[22]

Manfred Maier aptly characterizes the choice one confronts: we can accept and enjoy the illusions of cyberspace or we can dedicate ourselves to the development of the capacities and moral state of consciousness necessary to participate the knowledge of higher worlds. In this way we live our lives each day "between the light and the dark" worlds of supra-nature and sub-nature. It is our choice to do so in full awareness of the threats to our humanity, or to succumb to the sleep of media consciousness. Manfred Maier sums up the danger posed by the steadily growing array of media that dominate and define our ways of living as no less than an attack on the human ego itself:

> *All ego activity is being replaced by an immensely sophisticated, electronically concocted illusion, putting itself in the place of the ego and letting us dream . . . perhaps in concert with millions of others.* (p. 104)

Meeting Anthroposophia

The meeting/threshold experiences generated by the serious study of anthroposophy will have growing consequences for one's life and for the future of humankind. In addition to changing the way one perceives and thinks about oneself, the human community, and the natural world, one's deepening relationship to this path of knowing will increase one's sense of responsibility toward the developmental path of each. If this is the case for an individual, there will come a moment when a question arises within oneself: am I willing to take personal responsibility for the mission of anthroposophy in the world? As one reads Steiner's lectures and books one may encounter this question in various ways, but it may seem for a while that he asks it of another audience, of another group of listeners or readers, not inclusive of oneself. However, if one continues to pursue ever deeper meetings through one's study and meditative work, then one reaches a point when the question does not seem to come so much from Rudolf Steiner, speaking to an audience eighty or more years ago, but from Anthroposophy itself, addressed in a very personal way to oneself.

Taking responsibility in this deeper way for the work of anthroposophy can bring about a significant change in the nature of one's meeting/threshold experiences. It is not a summons that should be answered lightly or quickly. One should give the proper weight to the human tasks and responsibilities encompassed by this phrase "mission of anthroposophy." "Mission" is a term that in recent years has been over-used, which has left it with an almost clichéd shallowness. In the context of this pivotal question one should reinvest the word with the substance it deserves. In it one should hear the resonance of all that one has encountered in the course of one's study; one should hear the names of the leading figures who have committed themselves to it—Rudolf Steiner, Christian Rosenkreutz, Anthroposophia, the archangel Michael—and one should take into account the many others who have affirmed their relationship to the tasks encompassed by it.

One's affirmation can create the potential for an inner dialogue—a mentoring relationship—with the interlocutor who poses this question within oneself. Of course this is not the type of dialogue one is accustomed to having with a mentor—not even close. One should take care not to preconceive of such an exchange in the spatial, materialistic terms that have come to define our existence and limit or replace our imaginations of the intensive realm of the spirit. How does one engage in a dialogue with a spiritual mentor, or even know when it may be taking place? One's imaginations/expectations of spiritual reality are too often created for us by the fantasy worlds of film, escapist fiction, video games, or by the spiritual materialism inherent to some religious belief systems. As was said earlier in this introduction, when we first encounter anthroposophy we are likely to begin with a point of view that sees the spiritual realm as beyond the reach of our perceptual modality and therefore as unknowable in any direct way.

This is a type of "spell" cast over us by the bifurcated view of reality propounded by the scientific and religious orthodoxy of our time, which presents itself as the only rational, functional basis for modern consciousness and thereby the only rational point of departure for the shared perceptions that define our collective human existence. Whether one intellectually accepts this frame of reference or not, it has become a defining backdrop—a collective representation—that has a significant formative effect on our mental landscape and therefore on our conscious and subconscious preconceptions and expectations. In our everyday lives we conveniently forget how pervasively this orthodoxy shapes our perceptions of "extensive" and "intensive" reality. Our task or dilemma in creating a "state of consciousness" that enables a genuine intensive/spiritual exchange is to break this spell. Where should we look to find imaginations powerful enough to nullify the mental and spiritual impediments that stand in the way of this kind of meeting/threshold experience—in the way of a relationship with Anthroposophia?

In order to answer this question and to discern the process by which one can transform one's mental landscape and break free of the restrictions placed on one's consciousness by the orthodoxy of materialism, we would do well to turn again to Rudolf Steiner's early threshold and transformative experiences. It is not my intention to identify, as before, a particular revelation or epiphany, but to focus on the evolutionary process that prepared in him "the state of consciousness," or more accurately "the dynamic of consciousness," that would enable a working relationship with the special being who would become his mentor and who now serves as the bearer and spiritual persona of anthroposophy.[23] In other words, I want to return to the question that informed our exploration earlier, but ask it in a significantly different way: "How did Rudolf Steiner meet Anthroposophia?"

During the formative years of his twenties the two figures that stimulated not only his intellectual development, but also his spiritual advancement were Schiller and Goethe. We discussed above the influence of Schiller's *Letters* on Steiner's path of development, but what also played a formative role in the course of his life was an allegorical work by Goethe, *The Fairy Tale of the Green Snake and the Beautiful Lily*.[24] As with Steiner, Goethe found Schiller's *Letters* extremely provocative, most especially the delineation of the polarity out of which can arise a state of consciousness that enables the individual to become a free being. However, according to Steiner, "Schiller's solution was too abstract and narrowly philosophical for Goethe." (p. 91) After reading the *Letters*, Goethe felt impelled to create a work that literally would breathe life—the power of being—into these ideas and to depict in living forms the process of transformation of the human soul. To use once more Steiner's words to describe Goethe's intention in writing his *Fairy Tale*: "Ideas [must] become life-forces. We then have not just a knowledge of things, but we have made knowledge into a real organism, ruled by its own laws." Goethe would bring those ideas to life as the personae of an allegorical fairy tale, representing as a dramatic narrative the trials experienced by the human soul in its quest to regain its lost connection with the divine world of spirit. According to Rudolf Steiner, Goethe's own experience in writing this drama of the human soul was so powerful that it created in him a meeting/threshold experience: "while writing the *Fairy Tale*, Goethe had looked across the boundary, as it were, into the spiritual world."[25] Steiner was to make this observation more explicit in his lecture cycle on Rosicrucianism in 1907.[26]

Whereas Schiller's *Letters* had an immediate effect on Steiner, Goethe's *Fairy Tale* would take much longer. After being given a copy by his teacher Karl Julius Schröer in 1882 on his twenty-first birthday, it would be seven years before the artistic alchemy of the work would reveal its secrets to him: "it was in the late eighties of the last century that the knot of Goethe's *Fairy Tale* untied itself for me."[27] It is especially important, in light of the question—where do we find imaginations powerful enough to break the spell of materialism—to understand and appreciate the power of these imaginations, the dynamic, formative effect they would have on the biography and work of Rudolf Steiner. Also critical or requisite to the second question—how does one engage with a spiritual mentor—is an understanding of the developmental process that was "participated" by Rudolf Steiner during his seven-year meditative study of the *Fairy Tale*.

Evidence of the *Fairy Tale's* influence appears in all facets of Steiner's life. Arvia Ege in her essay "The Building on the Bank of the Stream and the Archetypal Structure of Community" draws our attention to the dramatic parallels between the artistic forms that come to life in the *Fairy Tale* with the physical architecture of the First Goetheanum and the organizational architecture of the Anthroposophical Society. As she clearly illustrates, the Temple that arises on the bank of the stream at the end of Goethe's allegory literally became through Rudolf Steiner the First Goetheanum. After its immolation, Rudolf Steiner would create the temple of anthroposophy anew even as he brought about the rebirth of the Society through a sacrificial deed that resonates with that of the Green Snake in Goethe's *Fairy Tale*.[28]

Literally through the biography and work of Rudolf Steiner a bridge would be built and made available to all humankind between the worlds of matter and spirit, establishing a clear linkage between the science of matter and spiritual science. Finally, the marriage that comes as the culmination of *The Fairy Tale of the Green Snake and the Beautiful Lily* could well be seen as emblematic of the spiritual union that was consummated at the Christmas Foundation Meeting of 1923 when Rudolf Steiner joined his destiny with that of the Anthroposophical Society, and thereby with Anthroposophia. During the seven-year gestation period, the imagery of Goethe's *Fairy Tale* was preparing the consciousness of Rudolf Steiner for what would be a steadily deepening relationship with this spiritual mentor.

To understand the generative dynamic at work through such imaginations, one must also consider the influence of another important inspiration cited by both Goethe and Steiner. In Goethe's *Fairy Tale* Steiner recognized a clear connection to the Rosicrucian stream of mystery wisdom. A month before Goethe reached his twentieth birthday, he became critically ill, coming close to death. His recuperation took almost two years, during which time Katarina von Klettenberg, a close friend of his mother, cared for him. In the course of his convalescence she introduced him to the literature of the mystical tradition and the Rosicrucian stream of mystery wisdom.[29] According to Steiner, on the basis of this near death experience and his exposure to Rosicrucianism:

> *[Goethe] had a momentous experience, passing through a kind of initiation. He was not actually conscious of it at first but it worked in his soul as a kind of poetic inspiration, and the process by which it flowed into his various creations was most remarkable . . . As time went on the initiation worked its way increasingly into his awareness and finally, as he grew more conscious of it, he was able to produce that remarkable prose poem known as <u>The Green Snake and the Beautiful Lily</u>—one of the most profound writings in all literature. Those who are able to interpret it rightly, know a great deal of Rosicrucian wisdom.[30]*

Through the imaginations of Goethe's *Fairy Tale* Steiner also experienced the power of this alchemical wisdom working in his own soul "as a kind of poetic inspiration . . . [that] flowed into his various creations." In the following quotation from Steiner's expository essay on *The Chymical Wedding of Christian Rosenkreutz* he describes what one can expect when working with numinous imaginations such as one finds in the *Fairy Tale* or *The Chymical Wedding*:

> *He who perceives in the spiritual world must know that at times Imaginations are assigned him which at first he must forgo understanding. He must receive them as Imaginations and let them ripen within his soul as such. During the ripening they bring forth in man's inner being the power necessary for understanding them.[31]*

Steiner, needless to say, is describing the transformational process that he experienced during his seven-year meditative study of the *Fairy Tale*. One can legitimately ask on this basis: who "assigned" him this particular set of imaginations? Could it not have been, either directly or through an intermediary, the being for whom the Temple "on the bank of the stream" ultimately was built to honor, Anthroposophia?

The imaginations of Goethe's *Fairy Tale* can serve as a kind of paradigm in answer to our question: where do we find imaginations powerful enough to nullify the spell of materialism? This is not to say that the *Fairy Tale* is the only, or even the primary place to look for such imaginations. Sources abound, in literature, in art, in the world's great religions, in folklore, and in the lectures and books of Rudolf Steiner, particularly in his four mystery dramas. Having answered this question, what instruction can we take from this prolonged meeting process of Rudolf Steiner's? Or in other words, how might one begin such a "dialogue" with the spiritual being Anthroposophia?

If one has sensed in oneself the question posed at the beginning of this section—am I willing to take personal responsibility for the mission of anthroposophy in the world—and one is working with it in the fashion suggested, one already has begun the dialogue. How, or in what form, should one expect to receive an answer or obtain guidance? If we take Rudolf Steiner's experience as an indication, one can expect a response— guidance—through all aspects of one's being. One's life path or direction will align more closely with one's ideals (willing life); one's capacities to work with others and empathize with their struggles or life situations, one's appreciation of the beauty, truth, and virtues that manifest through the medium of art and nature, all will grow more acute (feeling life); surprising insights will arise spontaneously in oneself from one's study, or in response to questions posed either by oneself or from others (thinking life). We seldom attribute such responses to a spiritual mentoring relationship because they do not come in the ways we expect, in ways that would satisfy our usual criteria of proof. Yet, these are the responses that change lives; this is the type of guidance that can lift one's humanity to a higher level. This is the type of spiritual tutelage that enables one to take responsibility for the mission of anthroposophy.

Steiner challenges us to sensitize ourselves to the subtleties of events and changes in our lives. He proposes a daily review of one's activity, with particular attention to occurrences that may signal a spiritual presence or influence. In many instances this influence may not be found in what happens in the course of a day, but in what does not happen because one has been diverted from an untoward event or situation. In short, in order to be fully attentive to the guidance of a spiritual mentor one must learn to read the signs in one's life, taking into account all three aspects of one's humanness.

Finally, two instances in particular stand out as opportunities for meeting and working directly with Anthroposophia: through one's collaborative work with others in creating—in a myriad of venues—the "healthy social life"; and through one's meditative work—regularly and rhythmically—with the Foundation Stone mantra. In both instances—to use Steiner's words—that which "unties the knot" or reveals its mystery is the formative dynamic that works through the archetypal principle of multiplicity in unity.

In her essay, Arvia Ege puts great emphasis on the responsibility of anthroposophy and the Anthroposophical Society, as a central part of its mission, to lead humankind in developing and spreading the know-how for building healthy communities. In "The Social Ethic Motto" Rudolf Steiner articulates the critical working principle that must become the heart of this effort:

> The healthy social life is found
> when in the mirror of each human soul
> the whole community finds its reflection,
> and when in the community
> the virtue of each one is living.[32]

In the context of the social life, multiplicity in unity becomes the practice of building the whole community in one's "I," while beholding one's "I" as most fully realized when it manifests in the wholeness of the community.

Multiplicity in unity comes to its highest expression in Anthroposophia. On the one hand, she bears in herself as a formative principle the highest manifestation of the human being, while her reflection of that imagination in the individual is expressed as one's unique higher self. Perhaps the most remarkable revelation about Anthroposophia is that she "has a deep wish to be spiritually present on the Earth in order to be able to work amongst [humankind]."[33] Since this is not possible, she dedicates herself to work in those who turn to her in order to bring to fruition the highest manifestation of the human being in them. The Anthroposophical Society is the community of such individuals in whom and through whom she wishes to achieve her wish.

Especially for someone who accepts personal responsibility for the mission of anthroposophy, the Foundation Stone mantra presents a set of numinous imaginations intended—or "assigned"—to create the "power" to work in this way with Anthroposophia. Through one's dedicated work with the Foundation Stone meditation, one can awaken the capacities to participate a direct knowing of the deepest mysteries of the human being. In so doing one can build this knowledge into all aspects of oneself, creating the "foundation" for the full realization of one's highest self.

> *The Ego of each individual is prepared to become the bearer of the Ego of mankind. The individual human being grows towards humanity; mankind lives as a whole in each individual.*[34]

In this way one raises anew in oneself the Temple "on the bank of the stream" within which one can realize—through making the sacrifice of the Green Snake—the fate of the Prince in Goethe's *Fairy Tale*, consummating one's ultimate meeting/union with the Beautiful Lily, Anthroposophia.

Notes

1 Calling oneself an "anthroposophist" usually entails being a member of the Anthroposophical Society; however, there may be those who are reluctant to join a public society where political currents and disagreements can arise, but who consider themselves to be part of the "anthroposophical movement" and thereby think and speak of themselves as "anthroposophists."

2 There are other considerations to be taken into account for one's difficulty in reading the lectures of Rudolf Steiner. The published lectures are based on transcriptions—sometimes multiple transcriptions of the same lecture from the notes of one or more stenographers—which Steiner did not subsequently edit. One can reasonably assume that there were gaps in some of the transcriptions and perhaps interpolations by the subsequent editors. Also, those of us reading the lectures in English, or languages other than the original German, must cope with the complication of translation. Certainly a scholarly analysis of these factors and their effects on one's reading of the lectures could be done. See for example, "Towards Understanding Rudolf Steiner's Use of Language and Structuring of Text," by Gerald Reilly, *Journal for Anthroposophy*, volume 71 (2000), pp. 28-37.

3 M. C. Richards (1916-1999) was a poet, potter and sculptor, painter, teacher, and author of numerous books including: *Centering, The Crossing Point: Selected Talks and Writings, Imagine Inventing Yellow, Toward Wholeness: Rudolf Steiner Education*, and *Opening Our Moral Eye*.

4   The modality by which spiritual archetypes, such as beauty, truth, and
    goodness, manifest within the ever-changeable, infinitely variable reality of
    the human being is consistent with what Goethe "saw" as working within
    the archetypal plant, i.e., "multiplicity in unity." See *The Wholeness of Nature*
    by Henri Bortoft (Hudson, NY: Lindisfarne Press, 1996) for a thorough
    discussion of this principle. Briefly, "the archetypal plant has the quality of
    diversity within unity . . . it is inherently dynamical and indefinitely flexible"
    (p.84). See specifically the chapters: "Goethe's Organic Vision," pp. 77-108,
    and "Seeing the Dynamic Unity of the Plant," pp. 261-290.

5   Rudolf Steiner, *An Outline of Occult Science* (Spring Valley, NY:
    Anthroposophic Press, Inc., 1972), p. 18.

6   For a comprehensive study of primal consciousness see Julian Jaynes, *The
    Origin of Consciousness in the Break-Down of the Bicameral Mind*, (Boston:
    Houghton Mifflin Company, 1976). Jaynes proposes that the mind of
    primal humanity did not exhibit a consciousness of self. According to
    him, there was no differentiation made or perceived between "self and
    other," between subject and object, no awareness of separateness that
    would arise from or be an indication of self-consciousness. He designates
    this state as the bicameral mind. The bicameral brain, he proposes, was a
    unified organ without differentiation into left and right hemispheres,
    otherwise identified with logical or analytical thinking (left brain) and
    creative or associative thinking (right brain). Jaynes contends that the
    origin of self-consciousness—the growing awareness of self as distinct
    from the world of solid objects and not-self—coincides with the gradual
    differentiation of the mind (or brain) into analytical thinking and
    associative thinking, into left and right hemispheres.

7   See Owen Barfield, *Saving the Appearances* (Middletown, CT: Wesleyan
    University Press, 1988), especially chapter VI entitled "Original
    Participation," and chapter XX entitled "Final Participation."

8   For a good introduction to Goethean science, see Henri Bortoft, *The
    Wholeness of Nature: Goethe's Way toward a Science of Conscious
    Participation in Nature* (Hudson, NY: Lindisfarne Press, 1996), especially
    chapter 2, "Making the Phenomenon Visible"; also, David Seamon and
    Arthur Zajonc, eds., *Goethe's Way of Science: A Phenomenology of Nature*
    (Albany, NY: SUNY Press, 1998).

9   For an excellent discussion of the study of anthroposophy as the first step
    in the process of initiation see Sergei O. Prokofieff, *The Heavenly Sophia
    and the Being Anthroposophia* (London: Temple Lodge Publishing, 1996),
    chapter I: "The Study of Spiritual Science as a Meeting with the Living
    Being Anthroposophia."

10 Rudolf Steiner, trans. Rita Stebbing, *Philosophy of Spiritual Activity* (New York: Rudolf Steiner Publications, 1963), "Second Appendix: Revised Introduction to the Edition of 1894," pp. 284-285.

11 A good source for such threshold moments in Steiner's life is the volume in this "Classics" series, *Meeting Rudolf Steiner*, selected and introduced by Joan Almon (Fall, 2005).

12 All references and quotes from Rudolf Steiner, *Autobiography: Chapters in the Course of My Life: 1861-1907*, Volume 28 of *The Collected Works of Rudolf Steiner* (Great Barrington, MA: SteinerBooks, 2006).

13 Johann Christoph Friedrich Schiller, *Letters on the Aesthetic Education of Man*, translation by Thomas Carlyle. According to the dated notes preceding the autobiography, Rudolf Steiner attended lectures on Schiller and Goethe given by his mentor Karl Julius Schröer in the year 1880.

14 The term "crossing point" comes from M. C. Richards, *The Crossing Point: Selected Talks and Writings* (Middletown, CT: Wesleyan University Press, 1966/1973). Specifically she is referring to the point at the center of the lemniscate, the geometric form often used to represent infinity. M. C. Richards uses this image as an imagination of the meeting of "two realms [that] are an organic breathing continuum," namely the realms of earth and sun (p. ix).

15 Also published as *The Philosophy of Freedom* (1964), and *Intuitive Thinking as a Spiritual Path* (1995).

16 For a discussion of the terms "extensive" and "intensive," see Henri Bortoft, *The Wholeness of Nature: Goethe's Way toward a Science of Conscious Participation in Nature* (Hudson, NY: Lindisfarne Press, 1996), "The Depth of the Phenomenon," pp. 68-77.

17 " 'Second Life' is an Internet-based virtual world video game launched on June 23, 2003. . . . Second Life Viewer enables its users, called "Residents," to interact with each other through motional avatars, providing an advanced level of a social network service combined with general aspects of a metaverse. Residents can explore, meet other Residents, socialize, participate in individual and group activities, and create and trade items (virtual property) and services with one another." (Wikipedia encyclopedia, 2008) Other program "clones" of Second Life are now appearing, including "Lively" from Google and "Home" from Sony.

18 William Gibson, *Neuromancer* (New York: Ace Books, 1984), p. 51.

19 The metaphorical use of "web" should not be lost on Internet users. One can be literally, not metaphorically, trapped in this electronic "web" even as the prey of a spider is captured, anesthetized, and ultimately assimilated. An interesting question to ask is what or who is the spider of this "web?"

20 See Owen Barfield, *Saving the Appearances: A Study in Idolatry* (Middletown, CT: Wesleyan University Press, 1988), Chapter II, "Collective Representations."

21 See for example Jeffrey M. Schwartz and Sharon Begley, *The Mind and the Brain: Neuroplasticity and the Power of Mental Force* (New York: HarperCollins Publishers, 2002).

22 See Clive Thompson, "I'm so Totally Digitally Close to You," *New York Times Magazine*, August 7, 2008, pp. 42-48.

23 For a thorough exploration of this special being as revealed by Rudolf Steiner, see Sergei O. Prokofieff, *The Heavenly Sophia and the Being Anthroposophia* (London: Temple Lodge, 1996).

24 Johann Wolfgang von Goethe, *The Fairy Tale of the Green Snake and the Beautiful Lily*, translation by Thomas Carlyle, illustrated by David Newbatt (Stourbridge, England: Wynstones Press, 2006). Also *Goethe's Fairy Tale of the Green Snake and the Beautiful Lily* (New York: SteinerBooks, 1979), with an introduction by Paul M. Allen and including "The Character of Goethe's Spirit" by Rudolf Steiner.

25 Rudolf Steiner, *Autobiography: Chapters in the Course of My Life: 1861-1907*, Volume 28 of *The Collected Works of Rudolf Steiner* (Great Barrington, MA: SteinerBooks, 2006), p. 94.

26 Rudolf Steiner, *Rosicrucian Wisdom: An Introduction* (Forest Row: Rudolf Steiner Press, 2005).

27 Quote by Rudolf Steiner from Tom Raines's, "Introduction," to Johann Wolfgang von Goethe, *The Fairy Tale of the Green Snake and the Beautiful Lily*, translation by Thomas Carlyle, illustrated by David Newbatt (Stourbridge, England: Wynstones Press, 2006), p. 15.

28 In re-founding the Anthroposophical Society, Rudolf Steiner accepted the position of president, a deed that previously had been forbidden to an initiate of his standing. In taking this step he put at risk all of his spiritual capacities and access to higher knowledge. See Rudolf Steiner, *The Christmas Conference for the Foundation of the General Anthroposophical Society* (Hudson, NY: Anthroposophic Press, 1990).

29 See Tom Raines's introduction to Johann Wolfgang von Goethe, *The Fairy Tale of the Green Snake and the Beautiful Lily*, translation by Thomas Carlyle, illustrated by David Newbatt (Stourbridge, England: Wynstones Press, 2006), pp. 7-19.

30 Rudolf Steiner, *Rosicrucian Wisdom: An Introduction* (Forest Row: Rudolf Steiner Press, 2005), pp. 3-4.

31 Paul M. Allen, ed., *A Christian Rosenkreutz Anthology* (Blauvelt, NY: Rudolf Steiner Publications, 1981), pp. 61-67. Also included in this anthology, "*The Chymical Wedding of Christian Rosenkreutz*: an essay by Rudolf Steiner," pp. 19-61.

32 Rudolf Steiner, translation by George and Mary Adams, *Verses and Meditations* (London: Rudolf Steiner Press, 1974), p. 117.

33 Sergei O. Prokofieff, *The Heavenly Sophia and the Being Anthroposophia* (London: Temple Lodge Publishing, 1996), p. 25.

34 F. W. Zelmans van Emmichoven, *The Foundation Stone* (London: Rudolf Steiner Press, 1963), p. 17.

What Is Anthroposophy?

Stephen Spitalny

Anthroposophy is a path of knowledge to guide the Spiritual in the human being to the Spiritual in the universe. It arises in a human being as a need of the heart, of the life of feeling; and it can be justified only inasmuch as it can satisfy this inner need. He alone can acknowledge anthroposophy, who finds in it what he himself in his own inner life feels impelled to seek. Hence only they can be anthroposophists who feel certain questions on the nature of the human being and the universe as an elemental need of life, just as one feels hunger and thirst.

Rudolf Steiner, *Anthroposophical Leading Thoughts*

Anthroposophy is the spiritual fount from which springs Waldorf education, the Camphill movement, biodynamic farming and gardening, Eurythmy, to name just a few of many scientific, artistic, and social initiatives. This name is derived from two Greek words, *anthropos* and *sophia* signifying "the wisdom of the human being," and expresses the lifework of Rudolf Steiner, 1861-1925, Austrian philosopher, scientist, lecturer, and author. Dr. Steiner spoke on a wide range of subjects out of a great depth and breadth of wisdom, leaving us a handful of books and thousands of published lectures. Since his passing, many others have taken up his indications in their own work, adding to the body of knowledge known as anthroposophy. Yet, the essence of anthroposophy is the activity of self-education through which one can come to know one's self and the world, an activity in which the human spirit probes into the nature of itself.

The basis for all of Dr. Steiner's work was his own path of self-development and spiritual research. He often advised not just to believe what he said and wrote, but to think about and meditate upon the ideas he brought, to do one's own spiritual research. Then one becomes active inwardly and one can come to know for one's self the truth.

Anthroposophy makes no claims to be the only true path; it recognizes truths found in other spiritual paths. Rudolf Steiner said: "there is only one truth, just as the view revealed from the peak of the mountain is the same for all who stand there. There are, however, various ways by which the peak of the mountain can be achieved."[1] There is no body of knowledge that we must agree with, no doctrine, and no set of lifestyle rules.

Self-directed activity is the key to this modern path of development. It can only be done from the inside. No one can do it for us. Both the questions and the striving for answers must arise within us. Although it is a meditative path, it does not separate us from the world, but, rather, enables us to live more fully in the world and be truly present in experiences, feelings, and thoughts. It is a path of awareness and attentiveness in all aspects of life.

This path of self-education leads to a transformation of *thinking, feeling,* and *willing,* the soul's basic activities. Our everyday *thinking* is scattered and based on sense impressions, but we can transform it into an active, living thinking that is more flexible and more self-directed. This relearning of how to think can be attained through disciplined, diligent effort. The transformation of our *feeling* life begins with paying attention to feelings: we experience and observe them objectively. This helps us to not be controlled by them, and at the same time to not deny them. Our *willing* is the most difficult to transform because it is the least conscious of our soul activities. The will, our capacity for doing, is ruled by instincts, habits, and desires, which we must first be able to observe objectively and then overcome. Often we act or speak out of ingrained patterns of behavior without thinking. We can strive toward choosing our actions instead of following habitual patterns of reacting. Taking up this active work on our own soul is a path of initiation leading to higher levels of thinking, feeling, and willing which Steiner described as *Imagination, Inspiration,* and *Intuition.*

There are a great many exercises that we can choose to practice on this path of initiation. They are not merely for our own development, but for the benefit of all.[2] Indeed, there is an inherent social element in the process of self-education. If we strive to make decisions and choose actions out of our highest intentions, then all of our social interaction may be lifted up to a higher level. Actions determined by our lower self separate us from other human beings; actions consciously chosen by our higher self serve to connect human beings. I believe this striving to raise our selves, our fellows and our world to a higher level is the essence of anthroposophy.

Rudolf Steiner promises us: "Insofar as we unite ourselves with the spirit of the universe, we become whole human beings, we receive impulses to search as human beings for the other human being, rather than pass one another by without understanding. The more we merely describe physical matter and then apply such descriptions to human beings, the more social life will be torn apart; the more we unite ourselves with the spirit, the more our hearts will open to other human beings. In this way, an education which allows the spiritual in the other human being to be found, provides the foundation for human love, human compassion, and human service, in the true sense of the word."[3]

Notes

1 *The Path of Knowledge and Its Stages,* 1906

2 See *Knowledge of the Higher Worlds and Its Attainment,* for an excellent introduction to some basic exercises.

3 Describing the ideals and benefits of Waldorf education in *Anthroposophical Pedagogy and Its Prerequisites,* April 17, 1924, Bern, Switzerland.

"Like Shadows We Are …"
(inscription on an old sundial)

Alan Howard

It is well-known to all who take up a study of Rudolf Steiner's *Philosophy of Freedom* that one of the first things to do is to get clear about the difference between percept and concept. One of the basic objectives of the first part of that book is to differentiate between the concept as such, and the concept of percept. The percept is the world of appearance only, what the world presents of itself to us just because we have eyes and ears, and happen to be there looking at it. We do nothing to bring that about. It just happens. All we need are healthy senses, and the world does the rest.

Were we only sense beings, however, this could never lead to *knowledge* of the world for us. It might lead to other results, as for instance a purely instinctive response, as it does in animals; but all possibility of knowledge would be out of the question. Something else has to be there for knowledge to arise, namely, thinking. Thinking seeks and grasps that other element in the percept, the concept or meaning. It is the concept added to the percept that makes the percept meaningful, and gives us knowledge.

So much is straightforward; but it raises two interesting questions. The first is: What is it that unites percept and concept in the act of knowledge? If they are so fundamentally different, as by definition they appear to be, what is it that makes them—once we have grasped them both—an indivisible unity? Why are they separate to begin with?

The answer, of course, is that *in themselves* they are not really separate at all, only to our perceiving and thinking. They are one and the same *thing*. The world is a unity. It is we who are "separate," in that perception and thinking are two separate activities in us. The world appears to us first of all in perception, and only afterwards—and not necessarily immediately—do we by thinking grasp what it is, the concept. Percept and concept in themselves, however, are both inseparably bound up with one another in the thing.

We have to do here with what is *for us* a distinction between the form, and the content or the meaning of that form. The form is all that is possible for us to perceive; the rest, the content, we have to get by thinking; but form and content in the thing itself are as inseparable as inside from outside, top from bottom. Percept and concept, then, are two ways of grasping the same thing; the percept by its very nature *compels* us to seek the concept, without which knowledge is impossible. The percept is really the *form of the concept as it is given to the senses*; but form and content are one in the thing.

Hair-splitting as this may seem (if not a little obscure, too), both Rudolf Steiner and Carl Unger draw attention to it in a larger perspective. If we take "seeing" to be what we generally understand by perception, then Light is the medium by which seeing takes place. But what is Light, really? According to Steiner, "In the universe we have light. … If we come out of the universe and regard it (light) from outside, what does it look like then? Like a web of thoughts. The universe from within—light; from outside—thought. The head from within—thought; from outside—light."[1] And according to Unger, "Pure thought is the supersensible element of Light; or, Light is the sense-perceptible expression of pure thought."[2] The concept, then, is the supersensible element of the percept, the percept the sense-perceptible form of the concept.

But all this has only to do with our *knowledge* of the world. That does not mean that our knowledge is the world. It is simply our way of grasping the world in accordance with such abilities as we have. The world as such, the "thing in itself" as Kant called it, might very well be different from our knowledge of it; and, because of our subjective limitations, even beyond our ever knowing what it *really* is.

So, the second of the two questions referred to above would be: What is our knowledge really knowledge of? Is it possible to know *that*?

Students of Steiner's work will not find this a trivial or fanciful question. Steiner himself often describes our knowledge of the world as something unreal, Maya, illusion even. Even our concepts, which are the very essence of knowledge, are, he says, only *shadows* of spiritual being and activity. He claimed that there was a more real, a "higher" knowledge; and what is more, one that it was possible for man to attain to. The problem, however, is: how can we have any assurance, on the basis of what we can already know, that there is such a "higher" knowledge?

This demands that we look a little closer at the knower—Man. He is not only a knower, he is a doer, too; and that which plays such an important part in doing is the same as that which is central to knowing, the concept (naturally, I am referring here to *conscious* human doing, not to a mere instinctive one); but whereas for knowledge the concept always comes *after* the percept, in doing it *precedes* it. In consciously doing something we "perceptualize," make visible to sense-perception, a concept which previously only existed in our thinking consciousness.

Now concepts, all concepts, are not things we create. They appear first in our consciousness it is true, and our consciousness being just that—ours—we identify ourselves completely with it. We believe we not only have "squatter's rights" in anything that happens in it, but we even believe that what happens there—at least as far as thinking is concerned—is something that we, and we only, have brought about. This is not so. Concepts appear in consciousness in the same way that percepts appear to the senses. The only difference is that we contribute nothing to the appearance of percepts; but we have to consciously work our way through to the concept by energetic thinking.

Following on from this, therefore, we can distinguish two kinds of concepts: *those that already have a perceptible form*, that is, those that are the meaning of the already perceptible world; and *those that have no perceptible form until we give it to them by something we do*. All inventions, for instance, all the wonders of our technical civilization, all works of art, indeed most of the things we do, were first concepts to which we have given perceptible form. They first existed *only* as concepts in the minds of the individual men and women who brought them into perceptible existence.

Our world then is a knowable reality by virtue of the concepts already implanted in it which thinking discovers. But our world is also a perceptible fact, a deed. If concepts, then, can only take on the kind of reality we are familiar with by being given sense perceptible form, "somebody" it would seem must have given them that form. There must be beings of thinking and will active in the existence of our perceptible world. They obviously aren't human beings; but although they must be infinitely superior to man, there is every reason for *believing* that they are nonetheless like man—or perhaps, better put, that man by virtue of his essential nature could be like them ("Let *us* make man *in our image*" said the Elohim at the foundation of the world). They are what spiritual science calls the hierarchies.

I have italicized the word "believing" above, because belief of course isn't knowledge; but belief which is well-founded can, and should be, the impulse to further knowledge. The reason why we don't have knowledge of such beings already is because they don't perceptualize *themselves*. They have no sense-perceptible form. We can only think them; and because we—that is, the modern world in general—have this dreadful hang-up about thought, that anything that is *only* thought cannot be real, we can only believe—or not believe.

But how, if we are convinced that our belief is justified, do we advance from belief to knowledge?

We have to realize that a knowledge which is limited to percept and concept cannot advance to knowledge of being. It can only rise to knowledge of things; and without knowledge of being we are no better off than the prisoners in Plato's cave.

Plato, you will remember, had this story of people imprisoned in a cave, and so fastened that they could only see the wall of the cave in front of them. Behind them, however, light shines into the cave from the opening, and throws shadows of all kinds of beings that pass to and fro across the opening (together, of course, with the shadows of the prisoners themselves; we must not forget that). These shadows are all the prisoners can *see*. They are their "world," their percepts. But being human, and therefore thinking prisoners, they will think about these shadows; and because they are real shadows they will be able in time to explain the laws of their behavior to one another. They will evolve a *knowledge* governing the behavior of this shadow-world; and because that knowledge will correspond in all respects to what is happening, it is easy to see that they will come to the view that this is not only the only world there is, but their knowledge of it is the only knowledge possible.

But it is still only a world of shadows. The beings who are causing the shadows remain completely unknown to them.

But are not we ourselves also prisoners in such a "cave," the "cave" of our consciousness? All we see are shadows, which the light of the world throws on the wall of that cave. These are our percepts; but because we too are thinking beings, we find they behave according to certain laws (concepts) which we discover in them. That is our knowledge.

And we need go no further. Many do not; but if we wish to do so then something has to be done about our way of knowing. We have to ascend from a knowledge of things to a knowledge of being.

In knowledge of things—percepts, "shadows"—we only need to find the concept that explains the percept; but for knowledge of being, especially a being that has no sense-perceptible form, it is a matter of transforming the knowing process. It is a change from knowing as an intellectual process, to knowing as a moral deed.

And that deed is Love; not love in any of the sentimental or self-seeking ways in which it is so often represented, but love as the selfless reception of another being. Love is giving up oneself to receive another being into oneself. It is the organ of cognition of being. The intellect can only take us up to the point where love becomes possible. Beyond that it has to sacrifice itself as intellect; and, emptying itself of self, let the other live, become known, in that emptied self.

Does that not already happen up to a point when we love another human being? Imagine you meet another human being. He is at first an object in space like anything else, a percept, in fact, a whole collection of percepts. You can think about those percepts, and eventually come to the concepts corresponding to them. In this way you can build up a whole library of information about him. All our anatomy, physiology, anthropology, and all the other -ologies have already done so. And very useful and practical information it is, too.

But not one single item of all this knowledge will ever give us the tiniest indication of what that being is to himself, what he is in his own essential individuality, what he is as "I." For that to happen one has to let that "I" come into oneself, and be itself there. That is Love.

And if this is true for another human being whom one can see, how much more so must it be true of those Beings we can't see. T.E. Brown, one of the minor poets of the nineteenth century, and therefore not so well-known today, puts this exquisitely:

> If thou could empty all thyself of self,
> Like to a shell dishabited,
> Then might He find thee on the ocean shelf,
> And say, "This is not dead";—
> And fill thee with Himself instead.
> But thou are all replete with very *thou*,
> And hast such shrewd activity,
> That when He comes, He says, "This is enow
> Unto itself.— 'Twere better let it be:
> It is so small and full, there is no room for Me."

Knowledge of things and knowledge of beings are polar to one another. The one is principally activity of thinking, the other of will. But they condition one another reciprocally. The conditioning agent is Feeling. Feeling is what makes us interested in things, and interest is the very first beginning of love. Just imagine how you feel about something in which you have not the slightest interest. You have *shut yourself up* against it. You won't let it *in*. Even better, imagine how a child feels. A child is more awake in his feelings, and has no hesitation in expressing them in the strongest term. "I *hate* sums!" he says, because all those facts and figures have failed to awaken any love for them. Knowledge of this kind is information only, abstract information. It only becomes knowledge for us when we develop a personal interest in that information; that is, when we give up part of ourselves to that information so that it can live itself out *in us*.

It is this feeling in knowledge which also goes beyond knowledge, and inspires belief. Belief stirs the will to further knowledge. We cannot get to *know* being, until knowledge has first led us to *belief* in being; and although belief still is not knowledge, it is the first step along that path to knowledge of being. It develops that new organ of perception which is Love, the act of the moral will which can empty the self of self so that another being may enter into it.

Knowledge of things also involves the will, of course; but there the will is more of a spontaneous, one might almost say, instinctive element. It is the will to knowledge itself which is an inborn part of the natural knowing being of man. I referred above to the *compulsion* which exists in the percept as the sense-perceptible *form* of the concept. The percept, one might say, *demands* the completion of its conceptual content. We can't help knowing under such conditions. True, *we* consciously exert our knowing will, but the impulse to do so comes from without. In knowledge of being the impulse must come wholly from within.

This knowledge of being is to the knowledge of things as reality is to the shadows of reality. We live among the shadows of reality. We spend our time understanding all we can about them. Indeed, we have become very proficient in doing so. But they are still shadows; and the danger is that if we do not do something to penetrate through to the reality that subtends both them and us, we are likely to become nothing more than shadows ourselves.

That inscription from an old sundial which I have put at the head of this article is not complete. It has a few more words to it. Completed, it runs, "Like shadows we are, *and* like *shadows* depart" (my italics).

There comes a time for every man when he enters into the realm of real being. At death he too "escapes," as Plato would put it, from this "cave" of shadows. A very great deal may depend, therefore, on how far he knows himself as shadow- or real-being before that time comes. And according to spiritual science he can only get to know that real-being of himself here on earth—in the realm of shadows. Getting to know that real being of himself on earth is the pre-condition for knowing the hierarchies, the shadow-*creating* beings of the cosmos, in the life after death; for the self-knowledge man achieves on earth, whether shadow or reality, is the self-knowledge he carries with him afterwards into the realm of cosmic being. And that must be so, for, after all, a man's self-knowledge *is* himself.

Darwin makes the remark that we are less blinded by light in awakening if we have been dreaming of visible objects. Happy are they who, while here, have dreamed of seeing. They will the sooner be able to endure the glories of that World.

From "Selected Thoughts" by Novalis

Notes

1   *Thought and Will*; Dornach, Dec. 5, 1920.

2   *Principles of Spiritual Science*; Chap. 2, "Natural Science and Spiritual Science."

The Geometry of Meditation

Ann Steward

The resolving of seeming contradictions of terms such as those in the title of this article constitutes one of the essential tasks of anthroposophy and its unique contribution as a spiritual movement. At the outset, when Rudolf Steiner gave the alternate name of Spiritual Science to the movement, he took this task upon himself in bringing together widely different and apparently opposed fields of knowledge and experience in the close relation of the noun and its adjective. He meant neither of the words in the pseudo and arbitrary sense in which they are often questionably combined, and he proceeded to substantiate his usage of them in many of his books and lecture cycles. One of the latter, which is definitively called "The Bridge Between the Physical Constitution of Man and the Universal Spirituality" might stand for many other lectures in which the physical and soul-spiritual, spatial and non-spatial, earthly and cosmic are presented in a relationship that is itself the lectures' subject. The "bridge" or connection in those lectures is physiological; in others it is historical, or philosophical or, as in the case of the present study, geometrical. The single lecture on which this study is based does not bear a paradoxical title, being called somewhat non-committally, "On the Dimensions of Space," but it introduces at once the disparate realms of man's existence, and it posits the problem to be considered in the question: How can the soul-spiritual in man, to which the Ego belongs, work upon the physical and bodily which is in space: how can something essentially unspatial work upon something spatial?

Of all the aspects of the dichotomy in man this one has confounded him the most. Dr. Steiner speaks of the difficulties involved, not in philosophical terms, but in those of man's own experience. "Man is conscious of his own soul-and-spirit, he is well-aware of how it works, for he is aware that when he resolves to move about in space his thought is transformed into movement by his will. The movement is in space, but of thought no unbiased person can assert that it is in space. In this way the greatest difficulties have arisen, especially for philosophic thinking." He discusses then several of the ways found, not to deal with the problem but to avoid it. The easiest way is to deny that the dichotomy exists, in spite of all evidence to the contrary, by asserting that all is material, or else, all is spiritual. This leaves the problem stand as it is, and it leads men into a cul-de-sac, either of argument or dogma, scientific or theological. A second way is to admit the difference and resolve it as far as a psycho-physical parallelism in which the twain never meet. A third, on the side of spirit, is the "aberration of spiritualistic attempts to bring it perforce into space," and on that of the physical, the use of drug or drink to escape into the non-spatial world without the Ego to which it properly belongs. No real answer is forthcoming from any of these evasions; all lead finally to the same dead-end of division.

The anthroposophical way of dealing with the question is, first of all, to take it out of the field of abstraction on the side of the spiritual, and of abnormality on that of the physical, and to look for the answer in man himself as a *human* being: to trace it there where it must exist since man does live in the two worlds at once, within the capacity of his universal human nature. One has only to follow a certain line of observation step by step to come to a point where one can see for oneself where it has led.

The steps in this way proceed through the three known faculties of man, willing, feeling, thinking, beginning in the realm of three-dimensional space. This is the dimension of our willing, for with this faculty, however non-spatial it is in itself as a force or faculty, we go into action, moving about in space, obeying its laws, conforming to its structure—in short, living in it. As to how this "living" takes place, Dr. Steiner speaks of the will, "albeit a thing of soul and spirit," as following the movements of man everywhere, in being their motivation, externally in space and also within himself in the fulfillment of the functions of his life. "We cannot but think of it in this way: when we carry out a movement with our will it adapts itself and enters into all the spatial movements which are traced, for example, by the arm or hand. The will goes wherever the movement of the limbs take place. Thus … we must speak of it as a quality of soul which can reveal itself in three-dimensional space."

This fact about the working of man's will in space, when thoroughly realized, throws an astonishing light upon the Act of Divine Will "in the beginning" as it is related in the Book of Genesis. The Creative Words, "Let there be … let the earth bring forth … let us make Man …" bespeak the Will of the Godhead at work in the Act of Creation from the non-spatial to the spatial, bringing *form*—that which has dimension—into existence by *movement*. ("And the Spirit of God moved upon the face of the waters.") At the same time a relationship between the two conditions was established. When later, in the event called the "Fall," when Man chose by his own will to live in this dimensional world of Space, he was bounded by it, yet a way out of it was left to him in the other two faculties with which he was endowed by that final creative decision of the Godhead, "Let us make Man *in our own Image*."

Proceeding from the will, Dr. Steiner asks a leading question, "Do all the soul-qualities assume such a three-dimensional configuration?" As the second step in our observation, he leads us to consider the faculty of feeling. He describes this at greater length with what he calls more subtlety of thought which feeling requires if we are to understand how it exists and carries on its activity in two-dimensional space, on the plane of symmetry. This observation is based on the activity of all man's senses working from two sides of a plane of section, which divides him into two symmetrical halves. The most apparent one is the crossing of the line of vision of the two eyes, but there is a connection between right and left in every sensation. Further, all feeling is two-sided in objective relationships. Through feeling the human being is related to other people or things or situations outside the self. It is true, feeling, can "move" one into action in three-dimensional space, but only the will is involved in it. In its own soul-nature, it is inactive, inclined to be dreamy, to live in a kind of shadow-picture internal world. In Dr. Steiner's words: "The life of feeling is really like a painting on a canvas—but we are painting it not only from one side, but both sides. Imagine that here I erect a canvas which I paint from right to left and left to right, and observe the interweaving of what I have painted from the one side and the other.

The picture is only in two dimensions. Everything three-dimensional is projected, so to speak, into the two dimensions."

It is interesting to note how the very language of feeling, as it has come to word out of its own nature, indicates levels or planes. In political parlance, for instance, right and left have been extended in their meaning to include all the ways one feels in this sphere of experience. In the field of psychology the direction is high or low, or inner and outer, in an elaboration of terms mainly derived from Greek, however ultra-modern their application might be. In the world of the senses the range is an extensive and intensive one of physical and psychical polarities such as warm and cold, sweet and sour, soft and hard which are freely applied to experiences of the soul.

In addition to what Rudolf Steiner calls the genius of language for find-ing its own exact expressions there is one of grammar in the few survivors of its original existence. In English there is that subtle shift from adverbs as modifiers of all active—or in this case we can say *willing*—verbs, to adjectives in the case of feeling, both of the senses and the soul. *To feel* is treated as *to be*, that is to say, as a qualitative state, certainly not as a three-dimensional one that moves about in space. Languages, which often have a wisdom greater than that of men who use or mis-use them, provide for qualitative distinctions and differences which philosophies ignore.

The consideration of feeling as a plane requires "subtlety" of thought to grasp the fact that it can exist in space without being spatial. Space must always be three-dimensional. Feeling has a relation to space as planes have, but this does not give it a third dimension. Once we *see* this aspect of the nature of feeling we are already on our way out of space though still in relation to it.

Proceeding from feeling to thinking we find that we cannot possibly speak of a thought as being in space. Again we must admit a relation to space since the brain is thinking's instrument and this occupies space, but we cannot conceivably attribute the constitution of the brain to thought. In thinking we are somehow in the world of space—but where? As a faculty thinking has the possibility of *extension*, hence it can be character-ized as one-dimensional, and as taking its course in the *line*. In mathematics the line is described as a continuous extent of length, straight or curved, without breadth or thickness—*the trace of a moving point.* These last words are precisely descriptive of thinking as a process. It might better be called process than faculty because it is so continuously in action—not action in space, however, rather away from it, in pursuit of a point, with only a trace of itself left in the line … Again the genius of language gives us an exact expression for the connection we are seeking in *line of thought.* Or, when in an argument our opponent's mind begins to wander, our own impatient: What's the point? Keep to the point!

The process of thinking thus takes us out of space when it leads us to the *point.* Mathematically this is non-existent in space, being defined as that which has neither parts nor extent, but position only. Position? Where are we when we reach position only? Nowhere in terms of space; still we *are,* we have being. In fact we have increased, or better, intensified our state of being in having reached a central point to which all lines of thought converge and all planes of feeling refer: in short, the I Am consciousness, the Ego, a non-dimensional self-existent entity, which is to say, a spiritual one. We have reached the realm or world or state, call it what you will, of spirit, which is adjacent to the dimensional one of space, having been led out of this step by step, using no more than the faculties we already have, merely observing them more deeply in their own nature, and following them where they lead in the direction of their own development. This direction is built-in, so to speak, *structured* in the very geometry of the universe and of Man. There has been nothing theoretical, or arbitrary, or abstract about the procedure; it has been one only of self-knowledge, self-awareness.

The Ego has been the point in Dr. Steiner's single lecture, and he ends with it, *out of space.* But it is itself a starting point! We might set out from it in any of the directions of Ego activity, in the use of its three faculties, but the one chosen here is *thinking.* Literally at the end of the line, at its point, we find ourselves in another field of thinking activity, the one Dr. Steiner calls sense-free thinking, or meditation. Anthroposophical meditation is no dreamy, bemused state of mind, brought about in the field of feeling rather than thinking. Both feeling and willing, which must become sense-free in the process, are a constituent part of it, but it is itself a *thinking* process. On the way from the ground up as we have traced it, willing and feeling fall away only in their spatial reference; in their spiritual essence as a soul faculty or force they are involved in it. Inactive in space they have all the more of their essence to contribute to thinking as it traces its way to points given for meditation. Anthroposophy abounds in such points; it is itself, in its content, a prolonged life—lifelong—meditation since all of its subjects basically provide, or indeed require, sense-free thinking. Meditation arrived at in this way presents itself as the next normal step to be taken in the development of our thinking activity. Its counterpart in geometry, the point, describes it precisely as the line describes thinking, for it is literally centered on a point composed either of words or images, not passively but actively. Call this a fourth dimension if you will, but with a clear understanding that it is *im*measurable in terms of space. Aberrations and abnormalities, in which the Ego is absent, are avoided in this kind of meditation because it is sequential, with no gaps or leaps on the path leading to it, and takes place in the realm of the Ego as its *own* activity, out of its *own* nature as a spiritual entity in a non-spatial world.

To return to our first statement: the seeming contradiction in the terms "geometry of meditation" has been resolved inasmuch as it has been shown not to exist. The worlds of the spatial and the non-spatial, the physical and the spiritual, are not antithetic but complementary: not worlds apart but contiguous. Freely we pass from one to the other in either direction, in the use of our inborn faculties. The philosophers who have pondered the transition as a problem through centuries have had the answer within themselves in their thinking about it. The "vanishing point" is not only one in the perspective of lines in space; it is also one within, where we go out of space entirely in our thinking. The very word *point* is so significant in both our outer and inner life that a recent dictionary lists eighty-four different usages of it. Is it not strange that men have applied it to so much knowledge and experience of their world, yet to so little of themselves?

In anthroposophy all self-knowledge is at the same time world-knowledge. We have already indicated a connection with the creation of the world "in the beginning" as an act of will on the part of the Godhead. But this creation was an end-product—we might even say a dead-end if we take into consideration the perishable nature of matter which alone is three-dimensional. From the marvel of law and order in the created world, the infinite number and variety of forms, and the innate intelligence of its creatures, we must assume a previous plan and purpose in a Divine Mind before the Creation began. A few decades ago a world-renowned mathematician and astronomer reached such a certainty through his science, and expressed it inclusively in the words, "The Universe is a thought in the mind of God," thereby making thought the antecedent of the deed, and an attribute of Divinity. Hence its non-spatial nature as a purely spiritual activity. In Rudolf Steiner's book, *The Philosophy of Spiritual Activity* thinking alone of the three soul faculties is presented as having the possibility of becoming free by very reason of its non-spatial nature. It alone can be or become universal. Feeling is purely an individual activity, which relates all its experience of the outer world to itself as the subject. In willing the reverse is true in that the subjective self is related to the outer world as its object. As in feeling, however, the relation is a limited individual one. Only in thinking is it extended beyond subject and object. "The highest level of individual life," writes Dr. Steiner in that book, "is that of conceptual thinking without reference to any definite perceptual content." Such thinking takes place in anthroposophical meditation. But it is not detached and isolated from such reference: rather it is the next configuration of thought already indicated in the geometry of the universe.

Lecomte du Noüy, in his book *Human Destiny*, speaks in this connection of "scales of observation" as that which "creates the phenomenon," thus suggesting that one scale might be quite different from another, and begin where another leaves off. His statement that "Every time we change the scale of observation we enter new phenomena" leaves the way open beyond the dead-end of the world and man which science today has reached. Du Noüy calls this the "end of our journey in the fourth dimension, Time." Obviously the only way for the evolution of Man to proceed beyond this end lies in his discovery of a new "scale of observation" in a spaceless, timeless world through his faculty of thinking, which leads him beyond their boundaries even while he dwells in Space and Time.

Art as Spiritual Activity: The Three Faces of Beauty [1]

Michael Howard

> *... if a person is ever to solve the problem of politics in practice he or she will have to approach it through the problem of the aesthetic, because it is only through beauty that individuals make their way to freedom.*
>
> —*Friedrich Schiller*

Is beauty a pleasurable diversion or a necessity to human life? In our age of utilitarian pragmatism it will strike many as romantic idealism to suggest that beauty has anything practical to offer to the urgent concerns of social life. Even in its traditional abode of the arts, beauty is no longer assumed by all to be necessary or relevant. Can there be any truth to Schiller's assertion that the problems of politics can be solved through taking up aesthetics? What possible relationship could there be between beauty and freedom?

This essay will take as its starting point the premise that at the heart of all the difficulties and tragedies in present-day human affairs we find questions about the nature of freedom. These issues surrounding freedom are many-faceted, requiring many approaches. We shall pursue beauty as one approach with a surprisingly practical significance. To this end we must find concrete evidence to support Schiller's claim that "it is only through beauty that individuals make their way to freedom." Let us begin with a deceptively simple question.

Is the color red beautiful? Whether we reply "yes" or "no," many people tend to interpret this question to mean, "Do you like the color red?" Are these the same question? Does our personal feeling of pleasure or displeasure define beauty? In everyday discourse we tend to use the term beauty to refer to whatever pleases us and ugly for that which displeases us. For example, we say, "this red is more beautiful than that red," meaning the one pleases me more than the other. There is a good deal to support the view that beauty is a purely subjective matter, that, indeed, "beauty is in the eye of the beholder." Thomas Aquinas declared beauty "as that which gives delight to the mind."

We might ponder what it is in the red, and for that matter in any color, which delights us and makes it beautiful. Do all colors share something in common which makes them all beautiful? Can we not speak of the beauty of yellow as much as the beauty of blue and the beauty of red? In the world of forms is there not the beauty of a curve as well as the beauty of faceted planes? How can different colors or different forms, each having their distinct character, all share in the attribute of beauty?

Color is not the physical pigment, nor is form the clay. Color and form are the spiritual qualities of warmth and coldness, expansion and contraction made visible to our senses through the pigment and clay. *It is our subconscious experience of the spiritual shining or resonating through the qualitative dimension of sense impressions that we call the beautiful. Beauty is another name for the spiritual within the physical.*

Noise is the antithesis of the beautiful in the realm of sound because it remains solely physical. Musical tones are likewise physical, but in addition they possess qualities which lift sound beyond the purely physical. Someone may like noise, but that does not make it beautiful; similarly, someone may dislike a piece of music, but that does not make it less beautiful. Its beauty lies solely in its ability to move us to feel inwardly buoyed up or weighted down, whether we like it or not. We can express our subjective pleasure or displeasure for something such as a color without introducing the concept of beauty. To employ beauty to express our personal preference only obscures and demeans its full meaning and significance for human life. *Beauty is the only concept at our disposal to speak of the more subtle but objective delight we experience with the perception of non-physical or spiritual qualities, e.g., the weight or lightness of musical tone or the warmth or coolness of color.*

Beauty is not the divine in a cloak of physical reality;
no, it is physical reality in a cloak that is divine.
Artists do not bring the divine onto the earth by letting it
flow into the world; they raise the world into the sphere of
the divine.

Rudolf Steiner

Beauty is an experience of the soul/spiritual as it shines through physical substance. However, our experience of beauty depends on an inner activity of living into the material medium in such a manner that the duality of physical and spiritual is transcended; in this way the physical is raised into the spiritual. The great diversity of the physical world originates from the diversity of forces and beings within the spiritual worlds and expresses itself through different qualities. The spiritual worlds are a unified reality, within which there is, nevertheless, a great diversity of qualities of being. The apparent paradox that the diverse qualities of colors and forms (e.g., warm/cold, light/heavy) all share in the beautiful is explained by the fact that they share a common spiritual origin.

Whenever we experience beauty we are raised into the spiritual world. We may be accustomed to interpret everything in our normal experience in exclusively physical terms, but the experience of beauty points beyond physical reality. Beauty does not originate in physical necessity; it serves no material purpose. The beauty of the different qualities of color and form become windows into the spiritual which underlies all creation, including our own humanity. In this sense, the beautiful qualities of the world can become a living proof of spiritual reality; the inner or spiritual rejuvenation that beauty offers us can be understood as spirit nourishing spirit.

Some people may challenge the value of attributing the experience of beauty to a spiritual world that is outside the scope of our conscious experience. Some might question: if there is an actual spiritual reality of which we are a part, how can we know it? Beauty may begin as that which gives us pleasure, but if we become interested in knowing the source of our pleasure, beauty can be understood as an actual experience of the world of spirit within earthly reality. The pleasure in our experience of the beautiful can be attributed to the fact that our soul/spirit resonates before the soul/spirit worlds from which it originates.

"Beauty is in the eye of the beholder" not because of our personal taste, but because the perception of the beautiful depends on the way we observe the world. If we hear only sound, see only pigment or matter and do not feel the quality of the music, the color, or the form, then we will not behold beauty. Likewise, if we only experience our personal reactions or associations, we may have feelings, even pleasurable ones, but these feelings pertain to ourselves and not to the qualities of the music, color, or form. Here also we do not behold beauty. The experience of beauty depends on the way we observe, on the quality of our inner activity. In this context our inner activity has three possibilities:

under-feeling	feeling	over-feeling
which is	in which	which is too personal,
too detached,	objective/subjective	too subjective;
too objective;	are in balance;	perceives the ugly
perceives	perceives the	
the ugly	beautiful	

We meet a triad of qualities, with two polarities balanced in the middle by the third. We can recognize in the activity of "under-feeling," an Ahrimanic quality and in "over-feeling," a Luciferic one. Relative to these two possibilities of "under-feeling" and "over-feeling," feeling per se is the activity of experiencing within ourselves the spiritual qualities belonging to sense impressions outside ourselves, or conversely, to know the spiritual qualities welling up from within ourselves with the objectivity of an outer phenomenon. The perception of beauty is possible only through a Christic form of spiritual activity. Just as virtue holds the balance between two vices, beauty stands between two forms of ugliness. In order to attempt a clarification of this controversial dichotomy between beauty and ugliness we will consider not only the way beauty is perceived but the way it is created.

For example, there is a beauty in thinking that is rigorously clear and accurate. A thinking that dazzles us with its cool clarity has a beauty of an Ahrimanic character. But if it lacks enlivening warmth, a sense of human relevance, then it becomes cold and deadening, its beauty withers and becomes ugly.

The spontaneous expression of feeling that has warmth and vitality can also be beautiful; its expansive warmth is the indication of a Luciferic influence, a Luciferic beauty. However, insofar as it lacks objective meaning and clarity, remaining a formless froth of enthusiasm, what was ripe with beauty becomes over-ripe, and falls into the ugly.

The spontaneous life of an expressionistic work of art such as a Kandinsky is beautiful. But the cool, cerebral abstraction of a Mondrian is equally beautiful. We have already established that there can be different kinds of beauty, such as we feel with different colors and forms. It should not surprise us to speak of different forms of beauty in relation to different kinds of inner activity. Behind the creative vitality of expressionistic beauty lies a Luciferic influence; behind the cool, precise beauty of abstraction is to be found an Ahrimanic influence. However, to the extent that the subjective beginning of expressionism is objectified or the cool objectivity of abstraction is enlivened through the warmth of individualized experience, then these two very different forms of artistic activity are saved from the one-sidedness of their starting point. It is the Christic activity of balancing the one quality with a measure of its opposite which transforms an ugly "too personal" Luciferic experience, or an ugly "too detached" Ahrimanic experience into an experience of beauty.

All qualities have a spiritual origin, but they can originate from different spiritual beings. As two vices form the poles on either side of a virtue (cowardice—*courage*—recklessness), the Luciferic and Ahrimanic qualities are the two sources of ugliness. They are the polar extremes standing on either side of beauty; they contribute something essential to beauty, but, by themselves, they constitute the ugly.

In his novel, *A Portrait of the Artist as a Young Man*, James Joyce expresses, through the voice of Stephen Daedalus, the following perspective:

> The feelings excited by improper art are kinetic—desire or loathing. Desire urges us to possess, to go to something; loathing urges us to abandon, to go from something. These are kinetic emotions. The arts which excite them, pornographic or didactic, are therefore improper arts. The esthetic emotion

(I use the general term) is therefore static. The mind is arrested and raised above desire and loathing."

The idea of proper and improper art might suggest a moralistic tone, but this concept is of critical importance—as prominent contemporary thinkers such as Joseph Campbell, Robert Bly and others have confirmed. Whether it is in relation to works of art or anything else, to be attracted through desire, as much as to be repelled with loathing, is to be unfree, by compelling us to possess or abandon it. That which grips us with loathing, even if we like it (horror films, punk-look), is commonly experienced as ugly. In the opposite extreme, a beauty that compels us to desire it is a false beauty. It may give us pleasure, and, in that sense, we may call it beautiful. But if it compels us with desire (pornography), we experience another form of the ugly—ironically, an ugliness that is commonly held to be beautiful. The ugly is that which leaves us unfree through desire or loathing; the beautiful is that which does not compel but allows and supports inner freedom.

What are the qualities that most often inspire an instinctive and, there-fore, unfree attraction? To be passionately driven by creative impulses, however exciting or even spiritual they may seem, is inherently unfree. Ironically, it is the Luciferic spirit which claims to be a "free spirit." The opposite is actually the case if the sense of freedom, the feeling of abandoned release, floods through us beyond our control. Similarly, wherever abstract principles of efficiency and order exercise their compelling influence towards a "cool" standardizing and "high-tech" streamlining, we have another beauty that becomes ugly insofar as we must conform to its demand.

Ahrimanic Beauty	Christic Beauty	Luciferic Beauty
is Ugly	is Beauty	is Ugly
because	because	because
through loathing	by neither	through desiring
we become unfree	repulsing	we become unfree
	nor attracting us	
	we remain free.	

As we should not apply the term *beauty* to mere personal preference, we should not use the term *ugly* merely to describe whatever we do not like. Just as beauty in nature and art is a way the spiritual reveals itself to us, so ugliness, too, is an expression of the spiritual. However, the ugly is a spirituality that leaves us unfree by binding us to the objective realities of the physical world (the Ahrimanic) or enslaving us to the subjective realities of our inner world (the Luciferic). As such, the Ahrimanic weighs us down with too much loathing, while the Luciferic buoys us up with too much desiring. These spiritual forces are necessary to human life but not in their raw or extreme form. It is not in avoiding the Ahrimanic and Luciferic, but in striving to weave and harmoniously balance them that we exercise our capacity to be spiritually free. To the extent that a creation arises through engaging the Luciferic and Ahrimanic qualities with a measure of freedom, to that degree will it be beautiful. In this respect, the grappling with the beauty/ugliness of the Ahrimanic and Luciferic forms of spirituality in order to find beauty through a Christic inner activity gives the experience of beauty a prominent role in the human being's capacity to become a free spirit.

When we experience the beautiful, in its Christic sense, we are not compelled by any physical necessity; freed from physical necessity, we become spiritually free. When we perceive the spiritual, if only in the cloak of beauty, we are more free than if we had no experience of the spiritual at all. This, in part, explains Schiller's claim that: "it is only through beauty that individuals make their way to freedom."

For us to realize the full relationship between beauty and freedom we must become conscious of the inner spiritual activity that creates the different forms of beauty. If it is the spirit of desire or loathing which compels us, we are spiritually unfree. Thus, the criterion by which we can determine something to be beautiful or ugly is the spiritual quality it possesses to support or hinder inner freedom. When we find something or someone beautiful, it is because we experience the spiritual in that thing or person. To the extent that its spiritual form compels us to desire or loathe it, making us unfree, its beauty becomes ugly, irrespective of whether we like it or not.

I leave the theme of beauty and ugliness with an unresolved question: Is something *inherently* ugly because it makes us unfree through loathing or desiring, or is it only ugly *as long as* we loathe or desire it? Is the experience of ugliness simply an opportunity to transform an unfreedom into freedom? In that case, does the ugly transform into the beautiful through our attaining inner freedom?

To concern ourselves with the mysteries of beauty is a task of the highest order. We cannot unveil her secrets through force, but we should not abandon all hope of ever understanding her. As a practical matter, it is with an earnest playfulness that we can strive to find the ways to weave together the enlivening warmth of the Luciferic and the objective coolness of the Ahrimanic so that they complement and harmonize each other. Through such activity we will create a beauty that enlivens and ennobles our full humanity.

Through beauty we develop our potential to become free creative spirits as Schiller envisioned. The above considerations offer no quick and easy solutions to life's challenges but they do outline a practical way in which beauty leads to inner freedom by transforming artistic activity into spiritual activity. If we see that the development of inner freedom is critical to resolving the social issues of our time, then beauty does indeed have a practical and essential role to play in human affairs.

Notes

1 This article is taken from a chapter in the author's book, *Art as Spiritual Activity: Rudolf Steiner's Contribution to the Visual Arts*, which was published by the Anthroposophic Press in 1998.

Goetheanism Resurrected In Anthroposophy*

Annie Heuser

Rudolf Steiner points to the relationship between anthroposophy and Goetheanism in the following words:

> The 19th century did not succeed in making erudite men into human beings. Goethe, however, was able to work his way through from erudition to a human world-conception, and so evolution must now go forward with the help of a Goethean impulse. ... We must learn to affirm Goethe's spirit as decidedly as the end of the 19th century and the beginning of the 20th rejected it. ... Then the path of spiritual scientific knowledge, which without question must needs be won, will become connected with the historical path of reawakening Goetheanism.

Goethe succeeded in working his way through from mere erudition "to a human world-conception," the cognitive foundations of which Rudolf Steiner was able to illumine. Thus he forged for himself an historical connecting link with the cultural life with which he found himself faced.

There now followed a re-awakening of Goetheanism which, on the part of Rudolf Steiner, demanded a sacrificial, lonely battle. When destiny led him to Weimar, where he was called to work in the Goethe-Schiller Archives, his heart was filled with enthusiasm. "Here are re-kindled all the ideas which we imbibed from our earliest youth about the most wonderful period of the German people's development," he writes in a letter, and goes on: "I am living right behind the Goethe house, and in the mornings when I go to the Archives I pass the house of Frau von Stein.

---

*Translated and reprinted from *Betrachtungen eines Erziehers (A Teacher's Observations)* by Annie Heuser with the kind permission of the Pilosophisch-Anthroposophischer Verlag am Goetheanum, Dornach, Switzerland.

For me these are very dear connections." But soon his experience changes. His co-workers at the Goethe-Schiller Archives are learned men: Hermann Grimm, Scherer, von Loeper, Suphan and others. In *The Story of My Life*, Rudolf Steiner characterizes these personalities. The Weimar of that time soon showed itself to him as the "mortuary of German greatness," where "there is unfortunately no one with whom one could speak about Goethe."

It is fearful to perceive the isolation in which Rudolf Steiner found himself in his understanding of the living Goethe—an isolation intensified perhaps later on in the Berlin period when he was surrounded by literary instead of erudite men.

But his Goethe work in Weimar brought him great joy. He writes of it:

> Each day brings me something new out of the papers left us by this unique spirit, and I am getting ever nearer to completing the picture that I have of Goethe. I come across thoughts and ideas of which I have said to myself: "Goethe must have said them," suddenly right there before me, actually written down by him. … Increasingly I see Goethe as the focal point at which the rays of all occidental world-conceptions and civilizations meet.

Now, there is a piece of writing by Rudolf Steiner from the Weimar period, entitled "Credo, the Individual and the All," that throws an interesting light on the problems with which he was wrestling at that time, foremost of which was the relationship between self and world. "I am only prepared to part with my consciousness of self in order to find it again in the object. But to cast it overboard, to submerge it in unending objectivity, that can never lead to knowledge," he says in one of his letters from Weimar. He strives toward an understanding of how man's individuality is grounded in the whole. He describes in a lapidary style how the separateness of the ego-man calls forth pain and agony of being, while the submergence of self in the object—dissolution into the universe—is a release. Yet: "He who never was an 'ego' can never comprehend the 'ego'; he who has never suffered cannot understand the joy that lies in the comprehension of suffering. … In order to die, it is necessary to have lived." Considered in this light, the following makes clearly apparent in which sphere of the universe Rudolf Steiner felt human beings to have their roots:

Credo

The *World of Ideas* is the fountainhead and moving principle of all being. Within it lie unending harmony and blessed peace. Were any existence not illumined by its light, it would be dead, beingless and without any share in the whole life of the world. Only that which stems from the *Idea* has a meaning for the universal Tree of Creation. The Idea is the inward clarity of spirit, sufficient *in* itself and *unto* itself. The individual, the particular, must contain the spirit within itself, otherwise it drops off from the Tree like a withered leaf, and was there in vain.

A man, however, feels and knows himself as an individual when he awakens to full consciousness. But with this there is implanted within him a yearning for the Idea. This yearning urges him on to overcome his separateness and to allow the spirit to come to life within him, to be in accord with the spirit. Everything that is selfish, that makes him into *this* particular, separate being, *this* he must cast away, slough off; for it is this that darkens the light of the spirit. What proceeds from the world of the senses, from drive, greed, passion, this and this only is the will of the egotistical individual. And so man must root out this selfish will in himself. Instead of this, *he* as a single being must will *that* which the spirit, the Idea within himself, wills. Let go of your own separateness and follow the call of the Idea within you, for that only is divine! What you will as a separate, single being is an insignificant point, in the circumference of the universal whole—a point fast disappearing upon the stream of time. What we will "in spirit," that is central, for it brings the central light of the universe to life within us; such a deed is not subject to time. If we act as single beings, then we close ourselves off from the closed chain of cosmic action; we separate ourselves off. If we act "in spirit," we find our way livingly into the universal working of worlds. Destruction of all selfdom, that is the foundation for higher life. For whosoever destroys selfdom lives in eternal *Being*. We are immortal to the measure that we have allowed self to die within us. This is the true meaning of

"Who does not die before he dies finds extinction when he dies." That is to say: whoever has not allowed the self within him to come to an end during his lifetime has no part in the universal life that is deathless; he has never existed, has had no veritable being.

There are four spheres of human activity in which man gives himself up fully to the spirit while destroying all self-centered, personal life: in the search for knowledge, in art, in religion, and in the loving devotion to another person in spirit. Whoever does not live in at least one of these four spheres, lives not at all. The search for *knowledge* is devotion to the universal in thought, *art* in beholding, *religion* in the depths and breadths of the soul, *love*, devotion with the sum of all our spiritual forces to something, someone that seems for us a being worthy of treasuring as part of the universal whole. The search for knowledge is the most spiritual, love the most beautiful form of selfless devotion. For love is truly a heavenly light in ordinary daily life. Sacred, truly spiritual love ennobles our being to its inmost core; it lifts up all that lives within us. This pure and holy love transforms all our soul-life into something closely related to the universal spirit. To love in this highest sense means to waft the breath of divine life into regions where usually only the most repulsive egotism and careless passions are found. We have to know something of the holiness of love before we can speak of piety.

If a man has made his way through one of these four spheres, from his separate singleness into the divine life of the Idea, then he has reached that for which the spark of striving was laid in his breast: his union with the spirit, and this is his true *destination*. But he who lives in spirit lives freely. For he has wrested himself free of all that subjugates. Nothing commands him except that for which he gladly suffers command because he has recognized it for the highest.

Let the truth become life; lose yourself to find yourself once again in the spirit of the world.

Now, it is interesting to compare this "Hymn to the Idea" (as one could call it) with the "Hymn to Nature" which Goethe wrote at the same period of his life: "Nature, we are by her surrounded and embraced ..." so begin the well-known verses.

It is characteristic of Goethe to perceive especially how man is embedded in nature: "... powerless to step outside of her, and powerless to enter more deeply into her." Rudolf Steiner, we saw, gives a picture of man's being in relation to the idea, to the spirit; Goethe points to man in saying of nature: "She has neither language nor speech, but she creates tongues and hearts through which she feels and speaks." Starting out from a true knowledge of nature, Goethe climbs to a grasp of the being of man. Rudolf Steiner's life-path leads from the spirit-world, which at no time was closed to him, to an experience of the world of ideas. Before he revealed the path to spiritual scientific knowledge which, as he said "must needs be won," he opened, in his *Philosophy of Spiritual Activity*, a gate, suited to the consciousness soul, to a knowledge of the world of ideas. Goethe's way, on the other hand, led from nature to spirit, in that he "found in nature spirit-reality." Out of these two symptomatic writings, there emerges the same effect of polarity that we find by comparing the two characteristic childhood experiences of Goethe and Rudolf Steiner: Goethe as a boy builds an altar out of nature's handiworks. It is reverence for nature which allows him to find the way to its Creator. He tells of this in *Truth and Poetry (Dichtung und Wahrheit)*. Rudolf Steiner tells in his *The Story of My Life* of the delight that was his as a boy in the cultivation of purely inward forms, visible to the soul's eye only, free from outer sense-impressions. It was geometry that gave him this experience. Not nature, then, but the frontier-land of pure thinking made it possible for Rudolf Steiner to strike roots into the earth and to build up his life's work, which then reached down as far into earthly depths as up into spirit-heights.

If one should seek an image for the different qualities of spirit in Rudolf Steiner and Goethe, as they emerge from these considerations, there can come to mind what has always been meant in speaking of the symbols Lily and Rose. And just because Rudolf Steiner united in himself the impulses symbolized in Lily and Rose, he appears to us today, against the background of his comprehensive lifework, as Friend of God and as Leader of Men.

The impulse of Goetheanism, upon which Rudolf Steiner lays so much stress, becomes clearly evident through what he says about the verses we have been discussing. "In this 'Prose-Hymn'," he says, "there is a wonderful inclination toward God, similar to that of the seven-year-old boy building his heathen altar out of nature's handiworks—but there is nothing of Christianity." However, Goethe does not remain stationary in heathenism. In the conception of nature that he developed in *Faust* and in the *Fairy Tale of the Green Snake and the Beautiful Lily* lives a new "impulse for the transformation of men, a striving for a new understanding of the Mystery of Golgotha."

Rudolf Steiner says: When a modern man wishes his heart to be touched in the same way as men were touched in ancient times—say, by tales of Isis—then he should allow Goethe's "Prose-Hymn to Nature" to affect him. "There echoes directly out of the secret depths of the universe what sounded forth for men long ago when they heard tell of Isis."

It accords with the character of modern man to grow conscious of his relationship to nature, so that he can take his chosen path from the ground upward. To live only in pure ideas, and thereby to neglect sense-perception, does not lead to reality. Exact observation of the sense-world, on the other hand, allows a man, if that be his striving, to mature also at the opposite pole of his consciousness, that is, in pure thinking. Such a striving toward the spirit certainly exists in the man of today who does not entirely subscribe to a soulless science and technology. Only too often, however, this puts him back into outworn and traditional ways of thinking and attitudes of living. He fails to notice that he is warming his soul with images, ideas and words that do not really penetrate the depths of his heart. Certainly they may arouse enthusiasm, but this extends no further than the feelings, or leads to one-sided impulses of will; the ego does not live therein; it does not make him creative. And that it is which really matters. For when, after a striving for knowledge, creative impulses awaken in a man, then he begins, clearly and strongly, to stride along a path which leads him to an ever greater clarity in his relationship to himself and to the objective spirit-world. The resurrection of

Goetheanism in anthroposophy means: to take the sense-perceptible world seriously in exact observation; to watch the formation of ideas in order to control the balance in them between sensory and moral elements (for only then does the "individualized concept" retain its spirit connection), and lastly it means: to purify feeling and will so that artistic powers of fantasy may be freed which can then, in the work of art, persuade the perceived material to speak out loud its spirit-secrets. The whole world can provide the material for the creation of such works of art, in whatever manner the individual may, according to his own character and destiny, relate himself with it: the poet serves the word, the painter serves the colors, and so on; the educator and social worker are creative in the very lives of human beings. What matters is that no one should advocate gods or ideas just because *he* happens to believe in them, but rather that, through the development of a living thinking, the material world may be raised the first step toward becoming spirit. Then the creative forces receive constant nourishment out of the fountainhead of the ego, and will become ever more capable of playing their part in the transformation of the material world into accordance with the spirit, and in making the spirit free.

Rudolf Steiner stressed that Goethe's eye was directed outward to sense-realities, but: "He was much too profound a spirit not to feel: This sense-reality is not in accordance with that in which man's soul can feel at home. It has to be refined and purified."— "I do not need," Goethe senses, "to be untrue to nature; all I need to do is lift up fallen nature by means of artistic form, so that in her own being she may be an expression of the divine."

Anthroposophy brings to man a knowledge which may correctly unite with his humanity without having "to be untrue to nature." The senses do not deceive, only the judgment deceives, says Goethe, and for this realm of judgment the anthroposophist must acquire the attitude of mind which can lead him to a renewal of his whole human being. Should he merely use the anthroposophical truths, which out of his research Rudolf Steiner could transmit, for the furtherance of his own natural capacities in this or that direction, it will lead him sooner or later to one-sidedness. A total culture of the human self means: to open up the fountainhead in himself from which creative impulses can enliven thinking, feeling and willing. This happens when the ego learns to live in pure thinking and to relate its concepts to the sense-perceptible world. It is then of secondary importance whether the creative person makes platters or dishes, to use an expression of Goethe's. How the creative forces activate themselves is decided by the destiny- and life-situation of the person. But to the awakening of these forces in the ego, only the search for knowledge can lead him; and it does so when this knowledge takes possession not only of his head, but of the whole man.

Goethe's conception of adult education, and the character of his method, have often been described, for example, in the significant essays *Goethe's Spiritual Stature* by Albert Steffen, in which the idea of Goetheanism as a pre-school for esotericism is developed. "To come to a standstill where Goethe stood is senseless," says Rudolf Steiner, "but without having digested him, and without stretching one's capacities to the full with the help of the driving power which he put into the world, no progress is possible."

Through Rudolf Steiner, Goetheanism was resurrected in anthroposophy. He who succeeds in making the impulse of this resurrected Goetheanism into his own inward life-impulse is protected from false paths into which a mere subjective feeling-comprehension of occult truths can lead him, and he is protected also from an abstract mental vacuum, which even acquaintance with the highest truths cannot fill, when these reach no deeper than the intellect. Anthroposophic attitude of spirit, within which the Goetheanistic impulse dwells, is defined in the significance of the final lines in Rudolf Steiner's "Credo": "Allow truth to become life; lose yourself in order to find yourself in the world-spirit," and by Goethe's words: "That which is fruitful alone is true."

Translation by Virginia Brett

Art as a Threshold Experience

Van James

As I stand before a blank white canvas on my easel I encounter a threshold; I have an experience of the boundary between sense-perceptible phenomena and supersensible revelation. If a work of art is to be truly successful it somehow retains this threshold character throughout its creation—for art is a threshold experience.

Before art became decorative entertainment it served a religious and deeply spiritual purpose. Art was at one time used for ritual, meditation, initiation, and healing. Painted cave sanctuaries, upright stones arranged as open-air temples, sand paintings and mandala images—all are examples of art that can bring about an encounter with the threshold. Rites of passage, reading the language of the stars and the elements, diagnostic and curative therapies, exercising and focusing consciousness in meditative practice—art was essential to all of the confrontations of self with world. For example, threshold experiences were common to medieval humanity, and the Gothic cathedrals with their architectural and sculptural forms, stained-glass windows, painted icons and murals, chanting, music, and ritual drama contributed to a total aesthetic, multi-sensorial experience that uplifted and promoted a transcendent state of consciousness. Even today, many indigenous peoples have direct access to such experiences through their art forms. However, since the beginning of the scientific era, self-awareness has created a chasm between what Schiller in his *Letters on the Aesthetic Education of Man* called the urge toward *form* and the urge toward *substance*. This gap in consciousness is often referred to as the abyss.

As we begin to have experiences of this gulf in the soul, fear, doubt, and anger arise. The Dutch painter, Hieronymus Bosch, was not unfamiliar with such abyss experience. Living at the beginning of the 15th century,

Figure 1-*The Tribulations of the Soul*, by Hieronymus Bosch, is one of four round pictures on the back of a panel painting called *The Flood*, in which the human soul is depicted in an encounter with the forces of the abyss.

and as a likely member of the heretic Cathar movement, he often portrayed hidden themes in his unusual imagery, themes that dealt with the threshold experience and the soul's abyss. One such painting is *The Tribulations of the Soul* (figure 1), first in a series of four pictures that included *The Soul's Enslavement*, *The Rescue of the Soul*, and *The Reunion of Soul and Spirit*. In this particular image the soul is depicted as a naked human figure surrounded by three hostile anthropozoomorphic creatures. One attacker grabs the distressed soul by the hair, the second claws at the chest, and the third creature trips its victim while reaching for his arm. Clearly an assault is made upon the three soul forces of thinking, feeling, and willing, which are centered in the head, heart, and limbs. All four figures are placed well below the horizon of the painting within a dark gash in the earth, within an abyss.

Rudolf Steiner said, "Fear ... must not stop one from falling into the abyss of one's individual self, for one climbs out of this abyss together with many spirits and one feels related to them; one is thus born out of

Figure 2- The left panel of the red etched-glass window, situated at the western end of the Goetheanum, was conceived by Rudolf Steiner as the soul's meeting with the abyss. (Etching of window motif by Assia Turgeniev.)

the spiritual world, but one has taken in death ..." (*Wahrspruchworte-Richtspruchworte*, p. 76) The death experience at the abyss is what allows a resurrection in spirit. "One loses oneself on entering the spiritual world, but one knows that one will find oneself again." (*Esoteric Development*, March 2, 1915)

In the left panel of the Goetheanum's red window, Steiner depicts in etched glass the human soul atop a precipice with three ominous-looking creatures rising up out of the abyss below (figure 2). Wilhelm Rath describes this situation in verse form as follows:

But first, before I further tread
Upon this steep and lonely crag,
I must extend my gaze to the abyss.
My aim must be to train myself
To look into the depths with balance true.
Courageously I must confess
It is mine own abyss whose night
Is nourished by the beasts
That rise up from the depths.
They are my share of dragon's force.
Who fain would rob me of my vision,
And robbed me unawares till now;
But from now on they shall be revealed.

(The Imagery of the Goetheanum Windows, p. 10)

Inner courage and balance of soul is required of us if we are to cross this threshold of self-knowledge so that we will not be lost forever within the abyss of being.

In the early 1980s I was on a panel of artists at the *Arts in the Image of Man* conference at Dominican College, where the poet Robert Bly pointed out that James Joyce observed this abyss experience in an interesting way in art. Joyce indicates in his autobiographical novel, *Portrait of the Artist as a Young Man*, how there is a gap between what he calls "proper and improper art." Improper art is of two kinds: one type of improper art is *didactic* in nature because it tries to teach us a lesson—a lesson we may not wish to learn. It is aggressive, in-your-face art that attacks in the tradition of the *avant garde* (a French military term). Didactic art works out of antipathy, inducing fear by means of violence. An example might be, to discourage drunk driving by showing graphic images of automobile accidents with dead and mutilated bodies of offenders and innocent victims. It isn't pretty, but it is true. Joyce calls the other type of improper art *pornographic*, not because it promotes sexual material, but because it prostitutes itself, sells itself by way of sentimentality and sympathy. It seduces the observer and draws us in by playing upon desires. This type of improper art might show a shiny new automobile in a spectacular landscape with handsome, happy people

Figure 3- Michelangelo's *David*, was begun in 1501, and represents humanity at the threshold of a new era.

enjoying life—obviously because of the car they own. It isn't true, but it is pretty. Both forms of improper art deny freedom by pushing or pulling the observer one way or another. Proper art is the *"thin line of quiet"* created by a dynamic balance between these two extremes. Proper art, however, is beautiful and true, a delicate threshold experience which carries one over the abyss of improper arts.

Rudolf Steiner also saw two dangers in the arts: on the one side, copying outer nature, and on the other, trying to illustrate ideals or spiritual experiences. Again, one is the urge toward form, the other is the urge toward substance. One direction solidifies into objective realism of authoritative impressionism, the other disperses into subjective extremes of fanciful expressionism. All creativity arises out of these two tendencies, and when a subjective-objective balance can be achieved between the two streams genuine art unfolds its magic.

In 1501, Michelangelo began his famous sculpture of *David* (figure 3), choosing to depict the shepherd boy and future king not in the moment of victory, as was the tradition, but before his decisive battle with the giant, Goliath. David looks left according to the medieval belief that God protects one's right but leaves one open to evil on the left. He awaits his fate with the mixed emotions of fear and courage expressed upon his brow and in the taut muscles of his body. Michelangelo portrays David metaphorically as a citizen of Florence, facing the city-states and foreign armies that in the artist's time threatened Florentine independence. David is also the representative of early Renaissance humanity, possessing all the gifts of the ancients, yet standing on the brink of an expectant and uncertain scientific age. He is fashioned according to the old Greek aesthetic, in a last glorious image of the god-like human being. He stands, anxious upon the threshold of a new era in which the divine in humanity will be lost. He anticipates the challenge that awaits as he gazes into the abyss that the unseen Goliath represents. For the last five centuries Michelangelo's *David* has served as a picture of the human condition on the cusp of a dawning onlooker-consciousness.

In Rudolf Steiner's colossal wood sculpture, *The Representative of Humanity* (figure 4), a new *David*, perhaps worthy of the next five centuries, is shown in movement, striding forward, now fully in the midst of the abyss. Between the contracting forces of the chilling abyss below and the expanding power of the fiery abyss above and around, the representative of true human potential creates a balance at the threshold of matter and spirit. Rudolf Steiner carved this wood group in a style he called expressionistic-impressionism, and, although he referred to his artwork as "just a beginning," one can see in it an attempt to find the freedom between form and substance, between didactic and pornographic art. In this way art is raised out of mere decoration and entertainment to a realm of spiritual significance. Art becomes what it is intended to be—threshold experience, a bridge across the abyss.

Figure 4- *The Representative of Humanity*, by Rudolf Steiner, was carved during and following the First World War. Referred to as *The Group*, this 36-foot tall elm wood sculpture depicts the threshold encounter of humanity's Representative with opposing cosmic forces.

A New Vision of Nature [1]

Joel Morrow

Part I

Many years ago, when I was a student, I lived for a time in a tiny hut in a forest. The hut was heated by a kerosene stove, but was still very cold at night, and lonely as the wind blew through the trees down to the frozen river. There I spent many hours studying, reading, trying to envision my life. One cold winter night, with such thoughts in my mind, I fell asleep. That night I had an unusual dream. I dreamt that I awakened in my hut, I sat up in my sleeping bag and it was morning. I looked out of the window into the forest. A feeling of wonder and exhilaration filled me. It was not just that the snow had melted, or that spring flowers were now showing through the dry leaves. Outside was *nature before the Fall*. It is hardly possible to convey how different nature appeared. Years later I found the picture again in Selma Lagerlof's "Legend of the Christmas Rose," in which a winter landscape is transformed for a family of robbers on Christmas Eve; but then I was miles from such images. I walked out of my hut (or rather crawled, it was so small) and tried to open myself wide, ever wider, to this new world. … It was like walking into a big Advent garden. But just as I was bending down to pick up one of the crystals, I woke up.

For years this dream haunted me, it was so real an experience. I came to believe that the very thinnest of veils hangs between our eyes and another vision of nature entirely. Many were the nights I would lay myself down in hopes that sleep would unveil that vision again. Alas, it never has! But now, after twenty years have passed, I realize that those days in that cabin were only a glimpse of something yet to come. They have planted their dreams in me as a seed. I felt somewhat like our old friend Adam (the one who married Eve) when he pleads to be allowed to return to Eden and the Angel says, "You will be recalled late and slow." Like old Adam, I have been cast out to till the soil, left to re-discover that vision of nature through a greater effort than I had anticipated in the dreams of youth.

More recently that journey has begun to take on more definition. Through the Goethean study of nature a pathway has been cleared through it; the presence of that invisible element which seemed to pervade my dream has begun to work into my consciousness again, however slowly. And occasionally I am even given the privilege of picking up a crystal and examining it for a while.

One of those crystals seems to shine through Bockemühl's discovery that a relationship exists between the cycle of the year and heredity. In his book *In Partnership with Nature* many chapters are devoted to how the plant is an expression of the cycle of the year, and how something infinitely mobile works behind the apparently fixed forms of nature. I was especially impressed by the "sub-chapters" in Chapter 3 entitled "Experiments to Broaden the Understanding of the Formative Forces in the Course of the Year," "The Year's Course as a Key to Understanding the Plant World" and "A New Perspective on Heredity." Bockemühl has shown that, within the year, there is a continuing series of gestures which can be described through the plants which grow in them. The plants make visible an interactive life which is the meat and drink of the biodynamic method. As one is drawn into the biography of the leaf forms, the mind, which at times seems to sit on life like a parasite, can become aware of what life really consists. Something in the mind goes down, like a setting sun, and arises again as a palpable, breathing connection to the spiritual form.

Hitherto I had felt a great dissatisfaction with the way biodynamic practitioners were able to express themselves. There existed a gulf between their own perceptual faculties and what they felt could be experienced on the basis of Rudolf Steiner's lectures on agriculture. Quite rightly, they plunged into a nature-experience and tried to create new instincts on the basis of interaction with the living world. Their feeling for biodynamics was profoundly tactile, which is as it should be. But I still felt there was something more to be discovered. It was as if they needed a new language, which was in accord with the kind of inward perceptual development that a serious biodynamic farmer would wish to undertake. In other words, *all spiritual development in the future might not be the same.* What may eventually live—in a modern form— as a Demeter wisdom may be quite different from the wisdom of other spheres of life. The foundations for that development must still be gradually laid.

For some time now I have pondered on what a farmer will look like when the future really occurs. I am not thinking of the technological farmer, who may also exist, but rather about a farmer who may have a true correspondence to the instinctive life of the peasant in times past. I am certain there are many important things missing in the world today, because certain kinds of people are not here to think them. I do not mean to idealize the peasant-farmer of old—his life was certainly very hard—but I believe he heard, out of his inseparableness from the land, something which for us *is silent.* Arising from the seasons, he heard thoughts which still had the force of will. They told him what he could do in his work and life that would still maintain his spiritual connection to nature. His habit of slowly walking over the fields had a meditative quality, for only slowly did these thoughts come to him. He had to wrestle them out of the stubble. Large thoughts came only with the passage of one season into another. Very intimately he read the "gestalt" of a restricted region. It might have been very important to notice his rhythm of work, probably an even pace, an economy of motion, as if each movement contained a thoughtfulness.

Actually, as I describe this peasant, I am seeing in my mind's eye the bent figure of Margarete Lueder working in her garden. She was very old by then and—God knows—she was not a peasant. But she assiduously cultivated their ethos. She wedded herself to their way of working, took up their rhythm and outlook and loved their relation to the land with every fiber of her being. She once said to me, "My love for those people has blinded me to all their faults."

The way she introduced me to biodynamic thinking was connected to the way she worked. Her meditative life was more responsive to the rhythms of the year than that of anyone else I have ever met. She did not think thoughts; she grew them. Because of this, the world looked quite different to her than to other people. I think she realized she had a task to fulfill in relation to creating a biodynamic view of the world, rather than merely a method, but this never dawned on me until recently, nearly seventeen years after she brought these things to my attention.

In her final years she was already living far-off in the future, contemplating a realm of free creative activity. She seemed to pass freely between the memories of peasant life (in East Europe and Mexico), which reached back into the last century, and a future state of human life, when nothing will be drawn from tradition at all. She described to me how all of us will pass through the eye of the needle, which is utter loneliness, and bring to birth a changing and fresh tonality of perceptions related to the cycle of the year. What the world is will be an *evolving moment*, whose truth will be to grasp the free play of forces which give rise to it, which are changing in the very moment of our grasping them. Truth will become mobile, just as is the world of growth and decay. Margarete Lueder was thinking such thoughts until senility made it no longer possible for her to think. But even in extreme old age it was surprising how she seemed to radiate health. The life of this old associate of Pfeiffer's was like an anticipation of something yet to come.

Part II

To approach this new vision of nature, an ever-increasing facility in grasping the life of the plant will be needed. For this purpose, the language of plant morphology is of great assistance. It must not be used, however, to increase our conceptual ability alone. It must change that conceptual ability, and make it more like the living world it contemplates. Speaking metaphorically, thoughts must become plants.

What is the living world, which our thought strives to apprehend? It is certainly inseparable from the cycle of the year which brought it into being. The cycle of the year is its origin and towards that cycle must our thinking wend if it hopes to become something more than itself.

Before I describe this, I would like you to imagine yourself standing by the ocean. Imagine yourself standing quite alone with the vastness of the ocean spreading out before you. You feel how vast is the expanse and how you are drawn out hypnotically into its rhythm. You watch the surf surge forward onto the shore with immense power. Then it withdraws again, back into the depths from whence it came. Its rhythm is like a giant breathing. Something inside you feels quite at home with this mighty force. You are carried into it, and though the ocean is the largest reality on the earth, you feel as if you are drawn into a dream.

Then, out of that vast dream, thoughts begin to swim into your mind, spawned by the great ocean. Why so it is! Does not that epic book of the ocean-experience confirm it? In *Moby Dick* one finds the words: "Posted like silent sentinels, stand thousands upon thousands of mortal men fixed in the ocean reveries. ... Yes, as everyone knows, meditation and water are wedded for ever."

Dear Reader, I beg you not to leave this shore as you contemplate the surging appearance and disappearance of the plant kingdom in the cycle of the year. If you can maintain the image of the ocean, you can feel that you are on the verge of another ocean of existence, as vast and as pregnant of thoughts as the ocean of water.

In Illustration 52 of Bockemühl's *In Partnership with Nature*, we stand before that tide within the plant world. The impression of this picture is of a giant wave, which reaches a peak at midsummer and then withdraws again. In this illustration twelve seeds of the same genetic type were sown in a greenhouse, one in each month of the year. Each plant shown is the same age. All have grown in a different time of year for two months. The effect of the entire series corresponds to the arc of the sun across the sky. The power of the ascending sun rises until June 24, and then tapers off dramatically after the July sowing. Bockemühl writes: "Seen as a whole the series reveals a formative movement of the year's course, out of which each individual form arises like a gesture."

The wave has a character. It expresses itself differently in the tops and the roots, as the season progresses. In the ascending year both the tops and roots branch extensively. By the descending year the gesture points like an arrow into the depths, with increasingly less branching above and below. Notice also the June plant, sown at high summer. Here the crest reaches beyond itself and expires at the moment of apogee.

These gestures can be followed further if the leaves from the above series are pressed and seen together. This is so in Illustration 59 (*In Partnership with Nature*). In each month there is a different dynamic between the tendency toward rounded leaves and rosette at the plant's base and the tendency toward indentation as flowering takes hold of the plant. The same seed type appears to be a different plant in each month of the year. Yet the series of differences is rhythmically connected.

The surprising discovery which Bockemühl made is that the range of appearances from month to month in a single groundsel type, which looks like twelve plants, actually corresponds to the range of type-variation in the species *Senecio vulgaris*. In other words, the fountainhead of types for each species is the sun's course. It would be wonderful to know if this is a law: that the change of light conditions throughout the year produce growth which corresponds to the array of the basic types within a species. Bockemühl is showing that genetic variations must always be weaving threads which are variations of the fluid growth of the whole. Each species and each type encapsule an eddy from the yearly flow and then play it out under specific conditions. In all of this a signature of the calendar can be seen.

One can see the yearly flow as the crest of a wave in Illustration 59. Follow with your eye the crest of each leaf series in a month. The crest is high and soon in midsummer and washes out far and low by late fall. It is like a tide. Stand before it in your mind's eye, as you did before the shore of the ocean. Just as the rhythm of the waves by the ocean and the experience of the tide have a quieting, thoughtful effect upon the mind, so also does the contemplation of the inflowing and outflowing in the rhythm of the year take us into another vast plane of existence.

As we stand by this shore, our thinking essentially changes its pace. We are before this vast ocean, which is washing at the shores of living existence.

Notice in Illustration 59 how only in the months of May, June and July has a certain completion of this process come about. The wave is high and short but also these are the months when the leaf-substance strongly tends to wrap around the stem, anticipating the fruit. By September it is washing out again with a low roar of surf. By October and November it is long and low and far away.

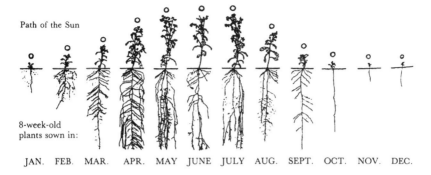

ILLUSTRATION 52
Greenhouse sowings of common groundsel from Bockemühl, *In Partnership with Nature*

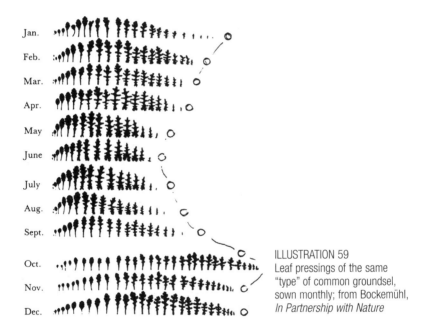

ILLUSTRATION 59
Leaf pressings of the same "type" of common groundsel, sown monthly; from Bockemühl, *In Partnership with Nature*

Carrying this image still further, one can see that, within this annual tide, what takes place to bring about the indented leaves has an active role, and with the rounded leaves a more receptive role. In the illustration, the indented leaves appear like the tide, the rounded leaves like the shore which is being lapped and shaped.

Each type of groundsel reflects a "moment" of the annual tide. Through this observation, Bockemühl removes from the realm of possibility the alleged *randomness* of mutation. These plant-pictures point to a whole, out of which the parts emanate. The reader is urged to work with these pictures in order to come gradually closer to the reality which they represent. I am certain that if such study were carried far enough, it could become an entrance into the non-visible workings of Biodynamics.

What seems to loom largest for the land-worker is how to take such thoughts out of the experimental sphere and to weave them into the life of the year itself. A farmer who meditates can have thoughts which immediately reflect his or her involvement with the cycle of the year. It is not only the plant which is washed by the annual tide. The human being is immersed as well and rides the crest to its completion every year. Just as he can feel the growth tendencies of each month, so also can he find thoughts which correspond and weave from the year into his inner life. He will want to find the spiritual correspondent to every seasonal movement.

With a certain steadfastness, he will be able to align his thinking to a seasonal rhythm, month by month. He will acquire the facility to banish from his soul what intrudes on this process. The year will grow in him and ripen, so to speak, into a Demeter-wisdom. The cycle of the year has always guided him in his work. Now it will give rise to an inner process. He must only work himself into this insight: "Just as the year brings about plants of specific forms, so also an oceanic tide of thought accompanies it. I must try to experience the shape of each wave, as it passes me by, immerse myself in its form, and experience its identity." Through this activity he will be able to develop that sensitive organ of nature-perception which Steiner calls the "Gemüt." Only when the farmer allows his "heart-understanding" to take the yearly tide as its source will the new vision of nature come into being.

Notes

1 Reprinted from *BioDynamics*, No. 148, published by The BioDynamics Farming and Gardening Association, Inc. Joel Morrow is the new editor and intends to make the magazine a forum for developing the awareness of nature described in this article.

An Anthroposophic View of the Heart Function

Guus van der Bie, M.D.

Forward by the Translator

Dr. van der Bie was born in 1945 in the Netherlands, where he is a practicing anthroposophic physician. The article which appears here in English, with the author's permission, was published in Dutch in Mededelingen der Anthroposofische Vereniging in Nederland, *December 1987.*

For an understanding of the background of this article it may be helpful to note the following:

At the founding conference of the General Anthroposophical Society in Dornach, Switzerland, from Christmas 1923 to New Year 1924, Rudolf Steiner presented a mantric verse, known as the Foundation Stone Verse, in which is condensed, as in a seed, all the essence of anthroposophy. Steiner said that the only right soil into which this seed could be planted was the human heart. It is this statement which prompted Dr. van der Bie to write the following article about the human heart, as he indicates briefly at the end.

A prominent concept in Steiner's thought, which can be found already in Goethe's work, is the idea of polarity: the relationship and interaction of qualitatively opposite tendencies. A case in point that Steiner elaborates from many aspects is the polarity of blood and nerves in the human body: the former being the essence of life-giving, building and regenerating processes; while the latter are the essence of life-consuming, conscious, but fatiguing processes that hover most closely near the boundary of death. Thus, while the blood is primarily engaged in processes which control our body warmth, nerve tissue is engaged in processes that are associated with the light of consciousness. It may be helpful to know that this polarity of warmth and light, mentioned in Steiner's Foundation Stone Verse, underlies some of Dr.

van der Bie's remarks, while the polarity between blood and nerve functions features prominently in his article. The polarity is worked out here in an original and objective way, using facts that modern cardiological science has brought to light and interpreting them in a spiritually scientific way.

Ernst Katz

In today's cardiology one divides the action of the heart into two phases. In the first phase, called "systole," all of the heart's muscle tissue contracts quickly. In the second phase, called "diastole," the heart muscles relax.

In the systolic phase we are to imagine that the heart muscle, after a period of relative inactivity, is suddenly activated. During this phase of activity one can distinguish a certain sequence of events originating in different parts of the heart, on a time-scale of fractions of a second. However from a macroscopic viewpoint, all of this activity can be represented as one sudden total event. The contracting heart appears as if struck by a sudden impulse.

The systolic impulse manifests in the heart muscle tissue, which structure differs from common muscle tissue. It has undergone a metamorphosis or restructuring, with the result that the functioning of this tissue shows a striking similarity to the properties of nerve tissue. In this nerve-like tissue of the heart we observe bio-electrical processes which are more readily understandable on the basis of what is known about the functioning of the nervous system than from what is known about the functioning of muscle tissue. The sudden impulse character of systole is caused in part by the nerve-like properties of this tissue. The impulse to contract is transmitted throughout this nerve-like tissue with utmost speed. Normal muscles contract much more gradually than the heart muscle. A typical muscle increases its tension gradually, as it were, until its contraction reaches a maximum.

During systole the blood vessels of the heart, the coronary arteries, are not filled, in contrast with all other blood vessels of the body. As a result the heart muscle tissue is to a certain degree bloodless during the entire phase of systole. In principle this is a life-threatening condition for the heart itself. Indeed, the vitality of our organs is directly dependent on being flushed with oxygen-rich blood. All normal muscle activity

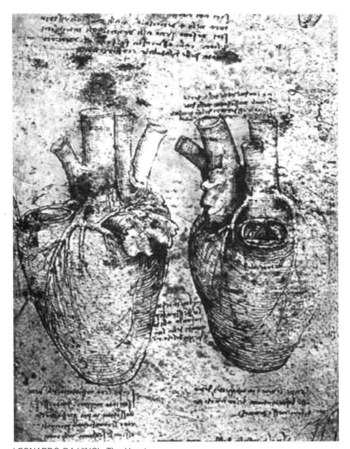

LEONARDO DA VINCI, *The Heart*

depends on a good supply and free flow of blood. In this sense the heart is an "abnormal" muscle. It combines contraction with becoming blood-less. It is true that a comparable process can be observed with our skeletal muscles to some small degree, but the complete contraction of the heart during systole approaches, as it were, a precarious condition for the heart. No part of the heart can escape this systolic condition, whereas skeletal muscles will contract completely in exceptional cases only.

In the polarity between blood and nerves, systole is evidently on the side of the nerves. Connected with this are some biochemical changes that take place in the heart during systole. The fluids of the heart muscle become more acidic during systole. Acidification in an organism is usually an expression of "astralization," i.e., activity. Our organism becomes more acidic, relatively speaking, during waking or intense work than during sleep or rest. The nervous system plays an indispensable role for processes of waking or working. During waking, the force of systole increases, as evident in our blood pressure. This pressure is lowest when we first wake from sleep, and it rises during the day as wakeful activity increases. A second fact worth mentioning here is the rising salt content of the heart during systole. Relatively large amounts of sodium chloride enter the heart muscle cells, which are thereby impregnated with salt. The nervous system is an extreme case of a "sodium chloride system." Its functioning is entirely dependent on sodium chloride processes.

Systole can be recorded by means of an electrocardiogram (ECG), which shows a distinctly articulated pattern. It is a characteristic feature of systole that this process can be recorded in minutest detail. Consequently one can distinguish in the recording of systole a normal from an abnormal one, as occurs with an irregular heart rhythm for example. When irregularities in the heart function are present, they tend to show up in the ECG as deviations from the normal pattern of contraction of the systolic phase.

Everyone sooner or later has a conscious experience of the functioning of his or her own heart, in the form of palpitations. What are these palpitations of the heart? They are conscious perceptions of one or more systoles. In whatever form the palpitation may appear, only the systolic phase can reach our consciousness. Insofar as our waking consciousness can expand beyond its normal bounds into the organs of the chest, it can, as far as the heart is concerned, *exclusively* reach only the moment of systole.

Systole is followed by diastole, or the relaxation phase of the heart. Let us adhere to the same order in studying diastole as we did with systole. The "nerve of the heart" is completely unable to function immediately after systole; it is then in a state of paralysis, which may be likened to the state of the eye just after it has received an image. Our eye is then blind for a moment (about one-sixteenth of a second). During that short interval of time we can see nothing, not even an intense flash of light. Similarly, for a short interval of time the heart nerve cannot be stimulated, and a renewed contraction of the heart is impossible. During diastole the coronary arteries fill with oxygen-rich blood and the heart is nourished.

The preceding bloodlessness of systole is suddenly contradicted in its opposite phase, and the improved flow of blood quickly eliminates the acidification and salination that resulted from systole. The heart recovers from systolic damage, so to speak.

The diastolic phase of an ECG shows a strong contrast to its systolic counterpart. While the systolic phase shows a detailed pattern, the tendency towards pattern formation is strongly subdued in the diastolic phase of the recording, which shows relatively little detail. Compared with the systole we can say: during diastole the *dissolution of form* dominates the function of the heart. This dissolution of form should be seen as the opposite tendency of what we have described earlier as the systolic tendency toward pattern formation.

Finally, consider the relation of diastole with respect to our waking consciousness. While systole can give rise to a conscious perception, diastole cannot achieve this. No situation is known, not even during disease, in which a person could become conscious of diastole. We might say: our state of consciousness during diastole is like our consciousness during sleep.

Let us now survey what has been described so far. When we list the characteristic qualities of the two processes described, we find that systole and diastole have completely opposite, mutually incompatible characteristics. They are processes which are each other's polar opposites, and thus represent two totally different effects in the heart. What then is "*the* true function of the heart?" It seems difficult to consider both systole and diastole together as a single function of the heart. Rather it seems justified to state that in systole the working of the nerve-sense-man becomes visible in the heart, while in diastole the effect of the blood-man becomes visible in the heart. The systole is thus interpreted as being not a function of the heart proper, but rather as the effect of the "upper pole" of man acting on the heart. Likewise, diastole can be seen as the effect of the "lower pole" of man acting on the heart.

Looked at in this way a space is created for recognizing what the true function of the heart itself is. This space lies *between* systole and diastole, *where the one polarizing process is led over into its opposite.* Here we find a possibility of describing the essential function of the heart itself. We shall call it "pole reversal," occurring from either systole to diastole, or from diastole to systole. Many times each minute our heart must overcome an immediate threat of death through polarization. *The heart accomplishes this by being the organ of pole reversal.* In reality this means that life originates in our heart neither during systole nor during diastole, but in the pole reversal. From that point in time, which we cannot record physically, but which we shall call for convenience the "point of pole reversal," life streams into our organism minute after minute. The heart can thus be seen as a most concentrated threefold organ. It is as if man as a being of opposite polarities reaches a culmination in the heart. And the quality of the heart raises the duality of opposites to a trinity by means of the process of pole reversal.

The point of pole reversal, between systole and diastole, deserves further study. Though this point appears to be of prime importance for the physiology of the heart, this moment evades recording.

We cannot easily find a possibility for getting to know this moment better if we confine our attention to the physical body of man. A consideration of music can help us to experience it. There, too, we meet with two entities which can be recorded: on the one hand, the rhythm which we may compare with systole, and, on the other hand, the melody as a series of intervals, which we compare with diastole. In making music as a creative artist we make use of rhythm and melody, but never do we identify true music with the playing of a melody exactly in rhythm. If the rhythm is applied rigidly the melody cannot come to life. However, the melody, as a series of intervals, can dissolve the rhythm, or at least modify it—make it more chaotic. When a musician plays music he finds himself in a non-recordable point "between" melody and rhythm! From this point the true musician creates the rhythm of his rendering. This is how the music comes to life.

The greater the artist, the greater is his capacity for living himself in the musical creation, so as to render what lives in it. At that moment the musician does not dwell on the physical plane. He dwells in a world of experience on a higher plane. What is experienced on this higher plane comes to life on the earthly plane by means of rhythm and melody.

If we make use of ideas such as these, they can help us to recognize also in other areas of life that each process which occurs rhythmically is in essence not of the physical order, but of a higher order, which borders immediately on the physical world. Therefore, each rhythmical process is a trinity that rises in its middle part above the physical order of things. Two phases may be physical, but the third phase never becomes physical. In this sense our heart connects us most strikingly with a non-physical world. Though biologists have long known that all organs function according to rhythmical processes, no organ is as instructive and exemplary in this respect as the heart.

The moment of pole reversal in the heart has properties which are of crucial importance for man's existence. From this point as a center of the heart function there streams into our bodily existence a renewal of life of undiluted intensity. By experiencing systole as a process of the upper pole, we can link it immediately to illness tendencies such as tendencies toward coldness, cramp, sclerosis, the "death in form." The healing process which the heart places over against these is a warmth impulse. This warmth impulse originates at the non-physical level of the heart process. It is a warmth stream of a non-physical nature. It is original supersensible warmth.

In diastole, as a process of the lower pole, we recognize another kind of illness tendency. It is a tendency toward loss of structure, dissolution of form. The threat here is the "death in chaos." The healing tendency with which the heart meets this condition is a light impulse. This impulse contains original supersensible light, which works down into the physical processes, creating forms and structures.

Looked at in this way, the heart can be experienced as an organ of the turning points of time. In man it is eminently suited as the organ through which the supersensible world can reach man, where man can bear the supersensible within himself. Through the trinitary nature of rhythmical processes we have in the heart a real bridge to the supersensible world. The heart can then be experienced as the dwelling place of Michael. The earthward route of anthroposophy passes necessarily through the heart of the human being.

The question why Rudolf Steiner laid the Foundation Stone Verse into the hearts of man was the motivation for this organ study.

Living Between the Light and the Dark: The Two Sides of the Electronic Media Experience

Manfred Maier

> *They have ears and eyes and yet they do not have the power of understanding through thought. The word of the prophet Isaiah is fulfilled in them: "You hear with your ears but do not understand; you see with your eyes but do not perceive. The hearts of human beings have become lifeless and dull. Their ears are hard of hearing and eyes are tired. In spite of their eyes they do not see; in spite of their ears they do not hear. They can no longer understand with the heart. Only if they change the direction of their inner life, will I be able to heal them."*[1]
>
> *From the Gospel According to Matthew 13:13-15*

This message from the spiritual world has come down to us through the ages. The Father God sent it through one of his Seraphim to the lips of His prophet Isaiah. The warning was intended for the people of Israel. Then Christ Jesus quoted these words to his disciples, referring to the multitudes.

At the end of his life in the very last of the *Michael Letters*[2] Rudolf Steiner characterized humanity's position between the Light and the Dark, spiritual and physical, in the following words:

> ... We must understand Sub-Nature for what it really is. This we can only do if we rise in spiritual knowledge at least as far into extra-earthly super-Nature as we have descended in technical sciences into Sub-Nature ...

> Only few feel as yet the greatness of the spiritual tasks approaching

humankind in this direction. Electricity, for instance, celebrated since its discovery as the very soul of Nature's existence, must be recognized in its true character—in its peculiar power of leading down from Nature to Sub-Nature. Only human beings must not slide downward with it.

The audience to whom Rudolf Steiner addressed these remarks knew very well the concepts that he here reiterates in an essential form. In the year 2000, however, we might re-examine the truth of these insights, recognizing how much more deeply humanity is enmeshed in the electric and electronic way of life now than it was in 1925. This is not a judgment, but a phenomenological statement of the reality in which we live.

We are called upon to seek a right knowing of our reality. Upon perceiving conditions that exude negative influences, we might feel the call to look for the forces of healing. Towards this end I offer the following comments.

Spiritual science has revealed to us that three events are fundamental to our time. Those events, which affect the whole of humankind and the destiny of each individual, are: the commencement of the Archangel Michael's Rulership as the Time Spirit in 1879; the coming to an end of the Dark Age, *Kali Yuga*, in 1899; and, the incarnation of Christ in the Etheric, the realm of Life enveloping the Earth, beginning in 1909. The totality of these events is basic to what Rudolf Steiner termed the *crossing of the threshold* into the spiritual world.

The subconscious crossing of the threshold of all of humankind seeks to become conscious in each individual. This reality manifests in the deep-seated hunger for living imaginations. Nowadays, this longing for the realm of the etheric is part of everyone's soul-spiritual situation, no matter how solidly it might be "buried," unrecognizable for regular day-consciousness.

If as children we receive an education engendered by artistic, scientific and religious involvement, irradiated by creativity, the warmth that comes forth from wonder and awe will nourish our budding forces of fantasy and imagination. Eventually, as we develop, we will feel a free and creative connection to the world that leads to the capacity to see the true value of things. One example is the ability to handle experiences such as the use of electronic media adequately. And as a major fruit of our education we need to feel enabled and nurtured to meet the pathways of our destiny with creative will.

At the very beginning of the new Michael Age, with the invention of the first efficient electric arc-lamp system in 1878 by C.F. Bush, and the incandescent lamp (light bulb) by Thomas A. Edison in 1879, the world started to become illuminated by electrically created light. In 1875 in the December 25th issue of *Scientific American*, Edison had described "an unknown *etheric force*" that became perceptible when sparks passed between carbon points at a distance from an interrupted electric current. As a result, he patented the "Edison Effect" in 1883 that would lead to the electron tube. Perhaps more significantly, Edison had already invented the phonograph in 1877 and the carbon transmitter, used to transmit sound into a varying electrical signal, which was to advance telephony significantly, in 1877-78. He spent the whole decade of the 1880s developing new mechanical and electrical ways to record and replay music.

These symptomatic events at the beginning of the Michael age indicate how a new dimension of sensory experiences was opening up that has continued into the present and has been intensified as the great onslaught on the senses that we are experiencing. The attack focuses especially on the visual and the auditory senses, but is not limited to them. Here the anti-Michaelic forces are revealed, working in the sub-earthly powers of electricity, seeking to divert us from the path to the etheric, the new and living light that became ever more accessible in the 20th century.

An ego-directed movement governs normal seeing and hearing if it is to become *conscious*; that is, *I* have to direct my eyes or ears to what I want to see or hear. I literally send my *I* out through the gates of the eyes and ears. Refined and guided, this is also a way to become conscious in the etheric.[3] This whole process generally, but not necessarily, falls flat when it comes to television. The eye and ear gates are purposefully targeted. All one needs to do then is not fall asleep and thereby not close the gates. All ego activity is being replaced by an immensely sophisticated, electronically concocted illusion, putting itself in the place of the ego and letting us dream for hours, perhaps in concert with millions of others.

I would suggest that exposure to audio influences is potentially more damaging than the purely visual. We see with the help of our eyes but we hear with our whole body. Regarding the visual, there is still a screen between the illusion-making powers and us, though this vision is far more captivating than regular seeing. In the process of hearing no such barrier exists. The soul is intimately close to the source of the experience. Rudolf Steiner said in 1923 that humankind would be able to overcome the purely mechanical fruits of civilization before it will find the inner-most impulses leading into the spiritual world. "But it is different with the *trivial* gramophone. With this humankind wants to force the artistic into the mechanical. If humankind becomes enthused for processes of which the gramophone is an expression, the help of the gods will be needed."[4]

When we are awake and fully incarnated we have two quite distinct experiences of our self. One experience is centered somewhat behind the point between the eyebrows and the other is the awareness of our whole body surface and the area around it, created by a conflux of the activity of our senses. Those are the manifestations of our central and peripheral egos.[5] In these two polar ways the ego-soul entity of the human being is incarnated, centrally in the head and peripherally in the rest of the organism, giving rise to a vibrating of one into the other and back again. During sleep, the self that is centered in the head excarnates; it becomes peripheral, while the peripheral self moves into the body.

When the movement function of the senses is not sufficiently guided by the ego but by electronic stimuli, our attention is focused for us and we are linked to suprasensory, sub-earthly forces. The peripheral ego, which normally serves as a shield when it moves in the senses, is cleverly circumvented and impressions sink much deeper into the organism.[6] This, in turn, lames the central ego that has no means to embrace the unending flood of often-disjointed impressions. It weakens and is in danger of losing its foothold in the physical-etheric body.

Our senses are also the gates for the most refined part of the threefold nutrition as it streams to us from the earthly and cosmic environment into sensing, breathing and assimilation of living substance. Firstly, the cosmic nutrition entering our senses maintains our body of life by providing the ethers of light, sound, and life and essentially making thinking, feeling, and willing possible.[7] Secondly, the digestion in our senses is the starting point for building up the substance of our whole body, except the central nervous system including all neurons. That part of our organism is really earthly.[8] The rest is cosmic substance. The senses perform their task within our warmth organism. They "remember" their origin in the very first phase of Earth evolution.[9] In this warmth the senses relate to the present sun-essence, continually created by and streaming towards us from the second hierarchy, the Exusiai, Dynamis, and Kyriotetes. We become conscious of this breathing through our senses when we dwell on an after-image and notice how the exhaling phase goes into the organism. All this can take place while light not only pours itself into the three dimensions of space, as it were, but also carries with it the radiance and warmth of a fourth dimension that Steiner calls *inwardness*.[10] It is this inwardness that makes light into a living cosmic substance. But what has life can die and decay and become something else. Rudolf Steiner taught that *electricity* is decayed light.[11] Now Ahriman[12] and his hosts from sub-terrestrial regions take hold of this decayed light and inspire all inventions based on electromagnetic forces. Human thinking enters these regions when we think materialistically. This is a necessary development in our age. So electronic media can be a wake-up call for the consciousness soul. The computer especially provides a spiritual reality for the human being to face. Our consciousness soul[13] has to gain strength to confront Ahriman and consciously seek the living ethers. If it fails to do this, it will be replaced by their counterparts, a kind of cold ether flowing out of electronic mechanisms. Slowly but surely they can choke off the etheric body, and with it the soul and the ego, from the living cosmic sun stream, that is, from the spiritual world.

Again, nothing should be said against electronic media. Rather, we understand that electronic media had to come. It is necessary that those influences exist. We, however, know that such a development needs to call forth the strongest forces of consciousness and conscience. In this light two of Steiner's remarks can be understood, namely, that the power of evil will come directly out of the forces of electricity,[14] and, that the etheric or life body related to the sense organization is being damaged in an extraordinarily strong manner through the assimilation of film.[15]

The investigation of microbiological processes in the brain has contributed a great deal to the understanding of how the electronic media influence and alter the developing brain. Also, influences of a psychological nature beyond physiological processes have been studied intensively by J. Healy.[16] However, to come to a Michaelic understanding of this matter we need to take into account the whole human being. All the scientific observations are extremely valuable if they can be deciphered in the light of spiritual science.

As a balance to the then starting development of electric and electronic media, Rudolf Steiner in Fall 1918, in a conversation with Jan Stuten, the genius musician and stage-designer at the Goetheanum, pointed to film as a future art form of great importance. He said that it would in a sophisticated manner answer the fundamental hunger for the world of images, of *forming* and formative forces. It would be extremely important for people to learn that anthroposophically creative artists could balance this powerfully arising pseudo-art with art-forms not delivered by an apparatus that would separate the audience from the human performer. The balancing art-form would creatively use means similar to film and would be a kind of "artistic play with light, music, speech, moving forms, and colors, produced by human beings in the moment." In the same conversation, Rudolf Steiner stated that film corrupts people's relation to space and time, kills the fantasy, harms the ether body, works against human freedom, and is therefore *magic*. It leads to obsessions and spoils the ability to have real imaginations.[17]

By way of conclusion I would like to give a short description of the Madonna Therapy, a healing practice that I feel to be a spiritually powerful, light-filled counterbalance to the attack on the senses. The Madonna Therapy was developed in 1911 by the physician Felix Peipers—together with Rudolf Steiner—for Peipers' patients in his Munich clinic. This therapy is so significant for us because it allows the eye, and with it the *I*, to dwell on a sensory/super-sensory impression intensely enough to let the stream of healing, inherent in the warmth of the inwardness of light, flow into our life body. The ether body is especially influenced by the impulses of art and religion. Rudolf Steiner speaks about the mighty healing goddess who, in a sisterly way, accompanied humankind from the most ancient phases of earth evolution, and who was called the "Holy Isis" in Egypt. This Isis is present with her healing powers in the picture of the Madonna with Child.[18] Since the ether body flows in the form of a pentagram,[19] the fifteen pictures, mostly by Raphael, are sequenced according to this five-fold flow. The child's position in relation to the Mother moves through the pictures echoing this pentagram in a living way. The series starts "in the clouds" with the Sistine Madonna and ends "in the clouds" with the transfigured Christ. This gives the life body wings, so as not to become too deeply attached to the physicality of earth existence, a danger we are all facing in the present.

In practice, the pictures are shown to a group as large prints or slides, while special music is played on the lyre. The series is available in postcard size. One can also meditate on them in the evening before going to sleep, allowing these images to flow into one's dreams. In them they surely will reveal a health-giving presence.

We live between physical and spiritual light and darkness. We have to go through the darkening of our physical senses to find the path to the spirit light. Without the fall into spiritual darkness, without its pervasive influence on our consciousness, we might not feel the need to seek to find the lost Isis-Sophia.

Notes

1 From *The New Testament*, a rendering by Jon Madsen, Floris Books, Edinburgh, 1991.

2 From his sickbed during the final months of his life Rudolf Steiner sent letters to the Members of the Anthroposophical Society. Into these he poured the distilled essence of his lifework in the Spirit. With other material, *The Michael Letters* are collected in *Anthroposophical Leading Thoughts*, Rudolf Steiner Press, London, 1973. See *From Nature to Sub-Nature*, pp. 216-19.

3 Rudolf Steiner, *How to Reach a Knowledge of the Higher Worlds*, Chapter 2.

4 Rudolf Steiner, Aug. 29, 1923, *The Evolution of Consciousness*, GA 227.

5 Rudolf Steiner, *Curative Education Course*, 1924.

6   Rudolf Steiner, *Cosmic and Human Metamorphosis*, Feb 27, 1917, Lecture IV.

7   Rudolf Steiner, *Pastoral Medicine Course*, Sept 13, 1924, Lecture VI, GA 318.

8   Rudolf Steiner, *Agriculture*, 1924, Lecture VIII.

9   Rudolf Steiner, *Theosophy of the Rosicrucian*, Lecture IX, "Planetary Evolution."

10 Rudolf Steiner, GA 291a, *Farbenerkenntnis*, p. 102 originally in GA 130, October 1, 1911.

11 Rudolf Steiner, "The Etherization of the Blood: The Involvement of the Etheric Christ in the Blood" Basel, Oct 7, 1911.

12 Ahriman, the leader of the angels cast down by Michael and his host. In ancient Persia's Zoroastrianism Ahriman was the opponent of Ahura Mazdao, the god of Light. He is identified with the devil that wants to bind humankind to earth. He is the spirit of cold intellect, the serpent of darkness.

13 *Consciousness Soul*, according to Rudolf Steiner, is the highest of humanity's soul capacities, which is undergoing a unique evolutionary development during this epoch.

14 Rudolf Steiner, Nov 4, 1917, GA 273.

15 Rudolf Steiner, June 5, 1912, question and answer session for an English audience printed in GA 303.

16 J. Healy, *Endangered Minds*, Simon & Schuster, New York, 1999.

17 Werner Schaefer, *Rudolf Steiner uber die technischen Bild- und Tonmedien*, Verein fur Medienforschung un Kulturfoerderung: Bremen, 1997, p. 121. *The reader should be aware that Rudolf Steiner saw a limited number of silent films.

18 Rudolf Steiner, *Cosmos, Earth & Man*, August 1908, first and second lectures.

19 Rudolf Steiner, *Das Johannes Evangelium*, Lecture II, Nov. 17, 1902.

The Building on the Bank of the Stream and the Archetypal Structure of Community*

Thoughts for the 50th Anniversary of Rudolf Steiner's Death

Arvia Ege

The following thoughts are related directly with the reality and deed consummated by Rudolf Steiner at the Christmas Conference in 1923 and have ripened slowly over the course of the ensuing decades to take form more as a gift of dawning realization than as anything which has been thought out or intellectually pursued. Since it is the aim of this Conference, under the title "Insight and Trust," to consider the meaning and function of the Free School for Spiritual Science within the General Anthroposophical Society, as it has arisen out of the impulse of the Christmas Foundation Meeting, they would seem to have bearing upon this theme. In attempting to formulate them here, hopefully with some degree of clarity, I must first of all express a deep debt of gratitude to an individual who first planted the seeds from which much which will be dealt with here has sprung.

This is a woman who had been a pupil of Rudolf Steiner's from the very early years, who became the leader of the Anthroposophical Group in Cologne, Germany, and then lived in Dornach for many years until her death in 1941. Her name is Mathilda Scholl, with whom I was privileged to study the basic elements of anthroposophy and the background of Rudolf Steiner's *Mystery Dramas* when I first came to the Goetheanum. She told me many incidents from the early days of the anthroposophical work in Berlin—as, for instance, how Rudolf Steiner had given her lessons in mathematics as a basis for her inner training; of

---

*Given at the New Year's Conference, 1975, at Spring Valley, New York.

his personal care of individuals who were ill; of his inexhaustible patience and lively humor; or of how, when a series of lectures was planned, he and Marie von Sivers had carried the bulk mailings to the post office together in a large clothes-basket.

It was she who first pointed out to me the hidden revelations in Goethe's *Fairy Tale of the Green Snake and the Beautiful Lily*, describing how, when the anthroposophical work was later centered in Munich, Rudolf Steiner had indicated a possible plan to perform it on stage. And then, a number of months later, he had suddenly, to her surprise, begun to distribute the text of the parts of his *First Mystery Drama*. At that time she had spent long hours copying out the parts for the various actors, while Rudolf Steiner wrote the dramas, handing her the text early each morning, even while the rehearsals were going on. And during the following years she made a deep study of the spiritual connections between the *Fairy Tale* and the *Dramas*.

Mathilda Scholl explained to me that Rudolf Steiner has shown that it is the mission of our present epoch to develop *community building*, community life; that it will be the mission of the next cultural epoch to develop *community organization*, through a deeper spiritual knowledge of measure, number and weight; and that it will be the mission of the epoch thereafter to develop a common, or *community consciousness*. Seeds for all of these, she pointed out, are to be found in the *Mystery Dramas*. But primarily these dramas represent an archetypal impulse for the goals of community life. They are a creative, spiritual germ, as it were, of cosmic potential for our present epoch. In our time, Rudolf Steiner has told us, it is now a question of the relation of the individual to the group, in such a way that each brings his particular contribution to the others through an understanding of his own karma, and freely places himself within the whole. The "law," which was given in the Egyptian-Chaldean epoch, regulating human life and human relationships outwardly, must thus be transformed in our epoch so that a *common* or *community life* is formed through the free action of each individual out of an awakening to destiny. In the next epoch, the development of a *common organization* will be the transformation of the Persian epoch, when there was a general regulation of human life through the Mysteries, in accordance with the rhythms and laws of the cosmos. And the further epoch, that of a *common consciousness*, will be a transformation of the ancient Indian epoch in Asia, led by the Seven Holy Rishis.

The impulses, which are implanted in the *Mystery Dramas* for these future epochs, flow, Rudolf Steiner tells us, from a great cosmic cultus which was enacted in the spiritual world under the leadership of that cosmic being of our times—the archangel Michael—at the end of the 18th century, a miniature image of which trickled through, as it were, in Goethe's *Fairy Tale of the Green Snake and the Beautiful Lily*. Thus the deep kinship and intimate interrelationship between the two.

*

With these words of introduction, let us turn now to the founding of the General Anthroposophical Society as the culminating deed of Rudolf Steiner's life, when he laid the foundation stone for the first free spiritual community of human beings for our epoch, laying this foundation stone in the heart of everyone who seeks to join it—and as its living token gave us the Foundation Stone Mantram. And at the same time he laid out the form, the architectural plan, as it were, for the structure of the Society—for this free community—consisting of the Society as a whole, with all its members, and of the Free School for Spiritual Science—two deeply interrelated entities, plus a small central group of individualities from whom creative initiative should flow—all of these established upon freedom and freely interrelated.

Ten years earlier, however, still another foundation stone had been laid, as we know—a double twelve-sided structure, which as a physical object Rudolf Steiner had laid at that time into the physical earth—the Foundation Stone of the First Goetheanum. And above it there rose over the years, through the labor of countless hands and hearts, that unique, awe-inspiring building of carven wood, consisting of two interlocking domes. These two circular structures, one larger than the other, opening into one another and forming, as it were, a great flowing lemniscate, had one central line of axis, from west to east. The traveler who entered from the west found himself surrounded by lofty columns which rose far up to support the great domes, while between them streamed light from vari-colored windows, etched with impressive images. Motion and life spoke everywhere from form and color. *Seven* great pillars on either side, with carven capitals and representing the stages of man's cosmic development, encircled him in the first larger half of the lemniscate, while the smaller circular structure, which lay before him, was enclosed by *twelve* pillars—at the central, farthest point of which, directly opposite him, was to have stood the great statue of the Representative of Humanity. Here the traveler would have beheld the Christ Being, striding forward to meet him, while holding the two great opposing world-powers in redeeming balance, through the free, powerful gesture of his arms—a gesture which permeated the entire building right into the very character of its forms. Under the loving gaze of this Being, upon the Stage which was surrounded by twelve columns, the *Mystery Dramas* were to have been enacted. And at the very center of the entire building, where these two circular worlds opened one into the other, at the convergence of the lemniscate, rose, when needed, the speaker's stand, from which Rudolf Steiner had already spoken ... and his words had scarcely ceased to sound, when the whole wonderful edifice was suddenly taken from the physical realm in a mighty pyre of flame, on New Year's Eve, 1922-23.

This building, in which anthroposophy had lived as a visible organism upon the earth, revealed in its whole structure and design the mystery which confronts modern man—his development from the past and the challenge facing him for the future. As master artist, Rudolf Steiner had embodied here man's origin and destiny, wrought work and active spirit—two distinct yet interpenetrating worlds within which he is called upon to awaken to himself, to his place within the whole, to his fellow men, and to his spiritual goal—worlds which here, visibly, opened freely and lovingly one into the other.

In this building the *Mystery Dramas* were to have been performed. It was built in a sense to house them, and flowed from the same source as both they and Goethe's *Fairy Tale*. Let us therefore consider the *Fairy Tale* more closely.

We cannot go into all of its marvelous details and varied characters, but let us consider some of its main motifs.

∗

Two Will-o'-the-Wisps, who have been brought across the stream by the Ferryman, scatter about them a quantity of gold pieces: light, which they have destroyed and turned into dead coins. And at the same time they learn, to their considerable annoyance, that the Beautiful Lily, whom they have come in search of, actually lives on the other side of the river across which they have only just come. In great dismay the Ferryman gathers up all the gold coins, so that they shall not pollute the stream, and throws them deep into a cleft in the rock. There the Green Snake finds them, quickly devours them with relish, and to her delight finds that thereby she begins to shine with a soft light which illuminates the objects about her so that she can see them. Within her the dead gold pieces are again transformed and begin to live once more as a new light. Hereby she is able to illumine the subterranean Temple, which she has long wondered about, and to discern the four Kings of different metals—gold, silver and bronze, and one of mixed metals.

"Whence comest thou?" resounds the voice of the Gold King.

"From the cleft in the rock where the gold dwells," answers the Snake.

"What is more glorious than gold?" asks the King.

"Light," replies the Snake.

"What is more refreshing than light?" he enquires.

"Human speech," she makes answer.

Whereupon there enters the Temple the Old Man with the Lamp. Its wonderful soft light illumines everything without casting any shadow, and it also has the extraordinary power to transform one substance into another, in accordance with deeper spiritual laws, as has occult insight.

"How many secrets knowest thou?" asks the Gold King.

"Three," answers the Old Man.

"Which is the most important?" asks the Silver King.

"The one which is revealed," he replies.

"Wilt thou reveal it also to us?" asks the Bronze King.

"As soon as I know the fourth," he answers.

"I know the fourth," says the Snake softly, approaches the Old Man and whispers something in his ear.

"The time is at hand!" cries the Old Man in a powerful voice. And at that moment both of them leave the Temple at the greatest speed—the Old Man toward the West and the Snake toward the East.

In the further course of events, the noble Youth appears who is also in quest of the Beautiful Lily—and at length the Snake, arching herself over the stream, forms a bridge upon which the Wife of the Old Man, the Youth and the Will-o'-the-Wisps are able to cross to the other bank. There, in a lovely park, attended by her three Handmaidens, they find the Beautiful Lily, who sits singing. But her song is sad, for she must suffer the lot to live always apart from others, due to the fact that she brings death to any living being who touches her—while to the lifeless she can give life. As she sings:

> *Oh, why is the Temple not yet by the stream?*
> *Oh, why then has the bridge not yet been built?*

the Youth, who is overcome by her beauty and finds it better to die upon her breast than to be forever separated from her, rushes forward to embrace her, only to die in her arms. Laying him on the ground, she stands as if frozen in utter despair, for she knows of no help. But the Snake silently glides around the body and, biting its own tail, forms itself into a circle, protecting the Youth from disintegration so long as the sun shines. Through the efforts of the others involved, the Old Man with the Lamp finally arrives barely in the nick of time, just as the sun is setting, and now protects the corpse with the light of his lamp. As the sun goes down, the light of the Snake and the soft glow of the veil of the Beautiful Lily mingle with that of his lamp as he says:

"Be quiet, lovely maiden. Whether I can help, I know not; one alone cannot help, but only he who unites with many at the right moment."

Joined now by the others, the assembled company keeps watch until midnight, when the Old Man looks at the stars and says:

"We are gathered together at a fortunate hour. Let each fulfill his role, each do his duty, and a common good fortune will dissolve within itself all separate ill and sorrows, even as a common misfortune consumes separate joys."

Whereupon, suddenly, each speaks aloud, simultaneously with the others, what he has to do, causing a ringing of mingled voices—the Snake begins to unwind itself, each begins to move, lifting the body of the Youth onto a basket—and an extraordinary procession now carries him back across the luminous arch of the Snake to the other bank, all shining in the dark of the night.

When they have arrived, the Old Man asks the Snake what she has decided to do.

"To sacrifice myself," she answers. "But promise me to leave no stone upon the land."

Turning to the Beautiful Lily, he then tells her to touch the Snake with her left hand and her beloved with her right. As she does so, life returns to the Youth—he arises, although his spirit is not yet awakened—and the Snake falls into thousands of precious stones. After gathering them all carefully together and throwing them, according to his promise, into the stream, the Old Man leads the company back again to the Kings in the underground Temple. And it is the Will-o'-the-Wisps who are now able to eat away the shining gold of the lock and thus open the door so that they may enter.

Here the words, "The time is at hand," resound for the third time. The Beautiful Lily cries out in joy—and suddenly the whole Temple begins to move. Like a great ship, it passes under the stream and, gathering speed, rises to unite with the Ferryman's hut, where it stands at last upon the bank of the stream. Here in the sun's rays, reflected by the hawk in the heavens, the spirit returns to the Youth, the three Kings bestow on him their gifts, giving him kingly status, and with an awakening cry, "But you have forgotten the fourth gift, the power of love," he is united at last with the Beautiful Lily. While in the meantime, over the stream a splendid bridge has built itself from the thousands of precious stones of the Snake's body, across which all the peoples of the earth now travel back and forth to the Temple from one shore to the other.

The whole action of this story and the movements of the Snake, who knows the fourth secret, form, as we may realize, a great lemniscate—the path, which the company travels from one bank to the other and back again across the stream, uniting two worlds. In each, very significant occurrences take place, while each individual character plays a particular part, lacking any one of which the final outcome could never be achieved. Viewed from one aspect, the movements of the Green Snake appear like the streaming of the blood in the human body through the heart to the lungs and back again to the rest of the body in a flowing lemniscate, indicating the mystery of the red and blue blood. But the aspects are manifold, for the motion is also cosmic.

And what is the fourth secret, which the Snake knows?

From her actions, as the story unfolds, we realize that it is the will to sacrifice herself.

In her answers to the Gold King in the subterranean Temple, the first three secrets are expressed: She comes from the rocks where the *gold* dwells. But *light* is more glorious than gold, and *speech* more refreshing than light. In these three, *gold*, *light* and *speech*, we can discover the secrets of man's development from *knowledge* to *imagination* to *inspiration*—the latter, audible in that speech which flows from, and can be heard in, the spiritual worlds, and which can stream from man to man and from heart to heart. But only when the fourth secret is known and acted upon, can the varied afflictions be healed, the single privations be dissolved in the one great good fortune, and the Temple rise to the bank of the stream.

This fourth secret, the power of sacrifice, of love, is also the power of *intuition*—the capacity to relinquish one's self, so that the other may live within us. In the deepest sense it is *death and resurrection.*—And we find this death and new becoming appearing again and again within the *Fairy Tale*: The original property of the gold which has been destroyed in the coin, the intellect, comes to life again within the Snake as a new light; the Youth who dies by the touch of the Beautiful Lily, is awakened to a new and higher existence through the sacrifice and mutual interaction of many who come together at the right time, and who in freedom speak aloud, in spiritual speech, what they have to contribute to one another and to the work at hand as they act for its achievement. The actions of the Snake, who bears the company on her back to and fro over the stream, and the touch of the Beautiful Lily on yonder side and on this—facilitated by the Snake—are interwoven in a marvelous pattern of death and resurrection.

As each participant—twelve in number—thus freely fulfills his destined deed, the hour of great good fortune arrives when the Temple rises from the depths. And the final sacrifice of the Snake, the manifestation of her secret, builds the bridge which enables the peoples of the earth to flock back and forth, linking one world with the other—the physical and the spiritual.

In Rudolf Steiner's *First Mystery Drama* these actions and characters all appear again—but now no longer as a fairy tale, but as an archetypal drama of our modern times, speaking to the consciousness soul in still more powerful images and import and sowing seeds for the distant future. Here we find again the Beautiful Lily and the Snake, appearing as the two Marias—through whom work, as Rudolf Steiner has told us, the two aspects of love and sacrifice: in Maria, the spiritual *light* of love, bringing death to the lower nature and life to what is dead—and in the Other Maria, the *warmth* of love, serving her higher sister through sacrifice. And here in the Sun Temple we find again the twelve, who, through having found their way to the Temple, and by freely giving there what they have achieved, make possible the further development and awakening of the others, as is heard in the words spoken there:[*]

> *So shall the cosmic goal be reached*
> *When each depends upon himself,*
> *And each gives to the others*
> *What no one asks of him.*

If we now turn our gaze back once more to the First Goetheanum, do we not find the same elements which we have just been describing, revealed within the whole structure of that building—the two worlds, united in the great lemniscate inscribed by the Snake and traveled by the assembled company, opening here before our eyes freely one into the other and visited by the peoples of the earth: the first edifice, the land of the gold; the smaller circle with the twelve columns, the realm of the Beautiful Lily, where each of the twelve participants who have gathered at the destined time *speaks* his gift to the others. May we not see in this building the Temple which has at last risen to the bank of the stream?

But after it was built, this House of Speech was taken from the physical earth in one night of fire. The Temple itself passed through death ... and through the culminating deed of its creator, the touch of his final

---

[*] From an early manuscript of the scene in the Sun Temple.

sacrifice, rose again to take on a new life. For is it not a further reality and mystery of the Christmas Foundation Meeting—the scope of which lies ever beyond us—that the whole form and substance of the First Goetheanum lives anew both in the Foundation Stone Mantram and in the form of the Society. In the structure of the latter, we find again two elements, two worlds, intimately related, opening one into the other— the General Membership and the Free School for Spiritual Science—both necessary to the whole: the School for Spiritual Science resembling the home of the Beautiful Lily, or the small cupola of the First Goetheanum with its twelve columns, where the Christ Statue was to stand.

This School is formed of its Sections for the activities of the arts, sciences and social life. Are they perhaps destined to be twelve? And at the heart of the School, as its spiritual life-organ, stands, in the architectural plan of its master builder—like the transformed Ferryman's hut—a central structure of three classes, where the light of transformation shines and the spirit speaks. And between the School and the Membership at large a constant stream of activity flows, where those with free, creative initiative serve in the common quest of all for that ever recurring moment when "The Time is at hand," and the event of the greatest good fortune can transform the single disasters and privations into new life.

The similarities and realities indicated here are so delicate and far-reaching in character that one hesitates to do more than touch upon them. But they bring into focus the theme of this present conference—*insight* and *trust*— so that we may perhaps attempt to draw the following analogies.

In gold, we have an expression of the first secret: knowledge, insight. Here the activity of the membership begins, striving for the transformation of gold into light, of *knowledge* into *imagination*—life-lit thought. At the other pole, the elements of *sacrifice* (the fourth secret) and of *speech* (the reality of the word) belong primarily to the nature of the School: training in the art of transformation for the common good—its highest expression, *intuition*. And inherent in the very nature of the power to sacrifice, we find, do we not, the capacity of *trust*. For trust is actually a giving. We *give* our trust.

And here perhaps I may quote a few lines by Karl Ege, written shortly before he died, when he was deeply occupied with the impulses for community.

"Rudolf Steiner tells us in the Youth Course," he wrote, "that trust between one human being and another is the greatest demand for the future—that, in the future, if we wish to become moral, upright human beings, then above all we must have trust in our fellow men. Trust must come to permeate all of social life. As we ponder these words, we can become aware that our putting of our trust in another human being springs actually from a hidden awareness of the higher nature within *him*, and our own capacity for trust from the higher being in *ourselves*. Basically, it comes down to trust in what is divine—the deep-lying awareness that the highest in others is of the same nature as the highest in us, that we all live and weave within the same spiritual reality—and that *reverence*—which requires an act of inner renunciation, of sacrifice—not I, but the other in me—lies at its core."

The thoughts which he expressed here lead us back to the considerations with which we started—to the relationship of one individual to another, and the group as a whole—to community building.

We recalled the fact that community building is the mission of the epoch which we are just entering, and that in the *Mystery Dramas* and the *Fairy Tale* the deepest impulses for this development are to be found. Further, we saw the wonderful correspondence between these and the First Goetheanum, where the same elements and activities are at work. And finally, we saw how these were born anew at the Christmas Conference, 1923—in the foundation stone and the form of the Society.

This deed of Rudolf Steiner's, in the little carpentry shop at Christmas, 1923, has been described as a deed on the highest spiritual plane, and thereby as a *seed* for all humanity. It has been entrusted to us as a structure to be built, with immense potential for the future. But it is a structure which reveals to us a particular *form*, harboring in its very nature all four secrets, and only possible of achievement when the fourth is exercised. It is the archetypal structure for the building of a free spiritual community of human beings on the earth. It represents the means by which such a structure can be built, if it is to be consummated—the basic spiritual form needed to contain such a community. And now we may realize the wonderful relationship between the Free School and the Membership—how they are indispensable to one another—and the great living mystery drama which takes place through this relationship.

And just as a deed, or impulse, which is archetypal can pour itself into number and quantity on the physical plane, multiplying itself like the "loaves of bread," just so, is not this archetypal form the fructifying kernel for all groups, all communities everywhere who will seek it and will take it into their active striving—as well as for the inner life of each individual?

Everywhere today, the coming generation is searching for community. Communities of every sort are springing up all over the world, although the greater part of them are foundering without a rudder, or on the verge of shipwreck. The need for community building arises spontaneously and with the greatest urgency everywhere in the modern soul. Yet is it not evident from the foregoing, and from what we see about us, that without knowledge of the spiritual and physical form and how to build it, without insight into the laws of freedom, as found in *The Philosophy of Spiritual Activity*—without knowledge and practice of the four secrets, it cannot be attained, and that the task of building it is a mighty drama.

Those who try to build it as a single separate circle of democratic equality and good will, based upon intellectual organization, or upon mystical dreams of unity and brotherhood, will not succeed—for they will only scatter dead coins and pollute the stream. The elements and means for transformation, for union with the Beautiful Lily, are lacking.

Here the great task for the Anthroposophical Society rises before us—for it has been entrusted with the secret of the form and substance of this archetypal vessel for the mission of our coming epoch—the structure which can rise from the depths, can pass under the river, through the thunder and lightning of the elemental world, to stand at last, together with its welcoming bridge, upon the shore of the heavenly worlds, its open secret accessible to all.

The thoughts which have been indicated here can only touch reticently on realities which are of dimensions potent for the whole of humanity. It is hoped that, from their very nature, it will be recognized that they do not attempt to do more than point to a few growing shoots of realization which have sprung from anthroposophy itself over a longer period of time. Perhaps the mood which imbues and emanates from them may be summed up in the question:

Is it perhaps possible now 50 years after the deed of Christmas 1923 and Rudolf Steiner's ensuing death, that we are just at the beginning of discovering what we have been given—the mystery of what has taken place, of what is to be the *leaven* of the epoch to come—and of *how* the "bread" is to become accessible to all who hunger for it?

In a lecture to the members in 1944, Albert Steffen points out—quoting Rudolf Steiner's own words—that, after the efforts for the Threefold Commonwealth failed in 1918—due to the strength of the opposing forces and insufficient human capacities—at a time when it might have been decisive in history and altered the course of events, Rudolf Steiner had given an answer to this failure—the answer found in the Christmas Conference, 1923. It was the fulfillment of the social impulse. Today, as we approach the end of the century, is it not borne in upon us more and more clearly, that, in the face of the worldwide disintegration which he saw ahead, Rudolf Steiner laid the foundation stone, the archetype, for a completely new form of social and spiritual life, which should spring up in the midst of the old and surmount its collapse—the mystery-work of the Green Snake and the Beautiful Lily, the Building of the New Mysteries on the bank of the stream with the bridge across, open to all— the continuously moving, recreative forms of the structure of a free community of human beings, which shelters not only the living, but the living dead.

Little by little, as we discern its contours more clearly, this task, which has been laid in our hearts and in our hands, beckons us ever forward; and we sense in this beckoning the wise gesture of Michael, summoning us to courage. And if, at times, the disintegration about us, the immensity of the task and our own shortcomings seem to all but overwhelm us, we may again and again recall and draw warmth and strength from the words of the Old Man with the Lamp, spoken when the Youth is at last united with the Beautiful Lily—words which refer to the fourth secret:

Love does not rule, but it builds!

Do *you* want to change the world?

So do we...

...from the inside out

study groups

LIBRARIES

threefold social forms

service providers   sculpture

Camphill communities   research

CONFERENCES

seasonal festivals   astrosophy

youth programs

Biodynamic agriculture

therapists   Eurythmy   ECONOMICS

architecture

Waldorf education   medicine   meditation

speech & drama   painting

consultants

PUBLISHING

In so many different ways,
members of the Anthroposophical Society in America are
actively participating in self- and cultural transformation.

Get to know us better by visiting our
website at www.anthroposophy.org;
email us at information@anthroposophy.org;
or by calling our national office at 734-662-9355.

Anthroposophical Society in America
1923 Geddes Avenue, Ann Arbor, Michigan 48104
www.anthroposophy.org   Tel: 734.662.9355   Fax: 734.662.1727

Contributors

ROBERT HILL is a writer and educator who, before retiring, served as President and CEO of Tunnell Consulting, an organizational development consulting firm. A former president of the Rudolf Steiner Institute, he continues to serve on its board as well as on the boards of the Triskeles Foundation and Biothera Pharmaceutical, a company dedicated to the development of products that improve immune health.

ROBERT MCDERMOTT, president emeritus and professor of philosophy and religion at the California Institute of Integral Studies, is editor of *The Essential Aurobindo, The Bhagavad Gita and the West* (forthcoming), and *The New Essential Steiner* (forthcoming). He served for twelve years as president of the Rudolf Steiner Institute and continues to serve as a member of its faculty. He was chair of the board of Sunbridge College and Rudolf Steiner College, and of the Sophia Project in west Oakland, CA.

STEPHEN SPITALNY has been a kindergarten teacher at the Santa Cruz Waldorf School for many years. A former board member of WECAN (Waldorf Early Childhood Association of North America), he has served as editor of their publication, *Gateways*, since 2000. Stephen gives lectures and workshops across the US and in Switzerland and has written many articles on early childhood education.

ALAN HOWARD taught Waldorf education for many years in England before bringing Waldorf education to Canada. In 1968 he helped found the Toronto Waldorf School, becoming one of its first teachers. In 1986, another Waldorf school opened in Toronto, and was named the Alan Howard Waldorf School in recognition of Alan's gifts to Waldorf education. Until his death in 1996, he continued to be a source of wisdom and inspiration to the growing movement of Waldorf education in Canada.

ANN STEWARD was a novelist, playwright, and poet. She wrote *Let the Earth Speak*, 1940; and *Take Nothing for Your Journey*, 1943.

MICHAEL HOWARD, a sculptor and teacher for over 35 years, is Director of the Life Form Studio in Amherst, Massachusetts. In addition to this work, he serves as an adjunct faculty member of the Barfield School of Sunbridge College. Michael edited and introduced *Art as Spiritual Activity: Rudolf Steiner's Contribution to the Visual Arts*, and is the author of *Educating the Will*.

ANNIE HEUSER (1896-1962) was a teacher of children (Berlin, Helsinki) and of teachers (Head Pedagogical Seminar, Goetheanum, Dornach, Switzerland) as well as a lecturer and painter.

VAN JAMES is a painter, illustrator, and graphic designer. He teaches visual arts at the Honolulu Waldorf School, is a faculty and board member of Kula Makua Teacher Training Program in Hawaii, and is a guest instructor at Taruna College in New Zealand and at the Rudolf Steiner College in California. In addition to teaching, Van serves as Chairman of the Anthroposophical Society in Hawaii, is editor of *Pacifica Journal*, and has written several books on art and archaeology including *Ancient Sites of Hawaii* and *Spirit and Art: Pictures of the Transformation of Consciousness*.

JOEL MORROW operated a market garden and greenhouse at Camphill, Kimberton Hills, PA., where he co-founded the Biodynamic Training Course. In addition to landscape gardening, he is a lecturer, and editor of *Biodynamics*.

GUUS VAN DER BIE, MD is an Anthroposophical General Practitioner in Holland. Previously a university teacher, he works part-time with "Goethean Science" at the Louis Bolk Instituut, teaching and writing for doctors and students.

MANFRED MAIER, who has a background in nuclear physics and chemistry, began working in curative education in 1968. He helped to develop "colored daylight shadow therapy," a unique sensory therapeutic approach pioneered in Camphill schools. Besides teaching science in the high schools at the Children's Village at Beaver Run and the Kimberton Waldorf School, Manfred teaches various aspects of anthroposophy, phenomenological study of light and color, geometry, clay modeling, and folk dancing. He also consults with organizations on sensory therapeutic work.

ARVIA EGE was a poet, sculptor and painter; she authored *Battle for the Sunlight*. Daughter of Percy MacKaye, Arvia was an artist and pioneer in her own right. She was among the early American anthroposophists living in Dornach when Rudolf Steiner was alive. Her entire adult life was devoted to enlivening the world through anthroposophical spiritual science. She founded the Adonis Press in 1941 and, in 1972, was a co-founder of the Hawthorne Valley ("Farm School") Association.